THE DAVID BECKHAM STORY

UNAUTHORISED & UNOFFICIAL

Ed Greene

First published in 2003

A CIP catalogue record for this book
is available from the British Library

ISBN 1 84442 770 6

Words:	Ed Greene
Design:	Matt Hicks
Photography:	Pics United
	Mirror Syndication
	David Brown
	Rex Features
	East News

Printed in Great Britain

THE DAVID BECKHAM STORY

UNAUTHORISED & UNOFFICIAL

Ed Greene

CARLTON
BOOKS

contents

introduction

They stand there waiting for him. The biggest club
in the world are about to sign the most famous
footballer on the planet. Sixteen years ago he came
to Spain as a schoolboy who dreamt of being a
professional player. Now, most schoolboys dream of
being him. As the money men and executives check
their watches, he steps on stage, ready to begin
another chapter in the David Beckham story...

the
boy
who
went
to
barcelona

The epitome of modern cool, it might come as a shock to his millions of adoring fans to discover that as a child David Beckham was something of a nerd. When it came to the staple youth pastimes of hanging around outside chip shops and going down the arcade young Becks was always conspicuous by his absence. Outside the hours of school and within the hours of daylight there's only one place you'd have found David Beckham... in the park kicking a football.

Born on 2 May 1975, in Leytonstone, east London, David Robert Joseph Beckham effectively grew up in a small recreation ground called Chase Park next to the family home in Chingford, Essex. Quiet, shy and relatively anonymous behind a school desk, with a ball at his feet young David came alive. Juggling it for hours on end, kicking it against a wall, taking shot after shot at goal, only darkness could bring a halt to these training sessions. His walls were plastered with pictures of footballers lovingly cut out from *Match* and *Shoot* magazines, and fanciful notions of becoming an astronaut or a train driver never entered his head. David Beckham only ever wanted to be a footballer.

That drive and ambition was in his genes. His dad Ted Beckham's business as a gas fitter paid the bills, but his passion was football. A half-decent player himself with non-league Barking, he had had a trial with Leyton Orient but never made the grade. So when David was born, Ted transferred his hopes and dreams of being a great footballer onto his only son. Ted may not have set out to create a super-player, but he was determined that if his son wanted to play football then he'd have had the best possible grounding. And young David didn't seem to mind.

"All I ever wanted to do was kick a football about," Beckham recalls in his (second) autobiography *My World*. "It didn't enter my head to do anything else. I know my skills come from working with my Dad in the local park. We would work on passing, crossing and shooting for hours and hours, from as soon as I got home from school until 11 o'clock at night all through my school days. The training he gave me as a kid has got me to where I am today."

But Ted wasn't just a football fan, he was a Manchester United fan. Despite being born and bred a Londoner, growing up in the days of the Busby Babes and suffering their loss in the Munich Air Disaster had sealed a place for United in his heart forever. Ted would buy David a new United strip for Christmas every year, and grandad Joseph (mum Sandra's father) was fighting a losing battle in his attempts to lure him over to his beloved Tottenham. Later, when he was invited to train with Spurs, David would famously turn up for every session in full Manchester United strip.

It was soon clear that not only was David going to be quite a footballer, but that this parentally-inspired dedication to practice and improving was something beyond the norm. One family friend, Don Wiltshire, recalls:

"When I first met David I asked him to juggle the ball with both feet. He only managed it a handful of times. I told him to come back when he could do it properly. A few months later he came back and did it about 2,000 times. He was that dedicated, even as a kid."

By the age of seven David was playing, and starring, in his first team. After being selected at open trials (one of 13 boys to make it out of 42), the future England captain was unleashed on the Enfield District League in the all-blue of Ridgeway Rovers. He was an instant hit. Rovers went unbeaten for the

David gets his picture taken at a celebrity match. Note the Manchester United tracksuit ... and, yes, that is Nick "Wicksy" Berry in the back row.

next three seasons and Beckham, playing up front, netted a staggering 101 goals in 115 appearances.

"David was a talent from the moment he started playing," recalls team manager Stuart Underwood. "He could score from 30 yards time and time again. He would take the free-kicks and we knew it was a goal from the moment it left his boot. I remember one game when he was 10 when he cooly chipped the goalkeeper from 20 yards."

As Beckham recalls in *My World*: "Even as a youngster I could kick the ball a long way, further than most other kids, and I scored twice for Ridgeway Rovers from the halfway line. I remember getting mobbed by my mates the first time. I absolutely adored training on a Wednesday night. Once, my mum and dad stopped me going to training as a punishment for something. That killed me. It was the worst punishment I could ever have had. They quite often grounded me when I wanted to go out, usually because I'd come in late, at 10 or 10.30 when they'd told me to be home by nine. Most of the time I did what they wanted but I stepped out of line sometimes, like most kids."

But Beckham wasn't like most kids. He had astonishing skill levels for his age and the kind of dedication coaches could only dream of. There was just one problem, his size. As Ridgeway coach Steve Kirby so neatly puts it: "He had legs like a canary."

Beckham was tiny. Arsenal scout Roger Smith, who regularly watched Ridgeway Rovers on his talent-spotting missions, remembers, "David was technically very good. But nobody could tell if he would fill out physically as he has. He was a good striker of the ball, but very weedy."

His size and love of United saw David nicknamed "Little Devil" at Chingford High School where he excelled at all sports, not just football – just as long as he didn't have to do any schoolwork. He played baseball, basketball, athletics, swimming and even rugby. He joined the cubs and went on a camp and remembers trips to the seaside at Southend, swimming in the sea.

"It was great fun," he says in *My World*, "but it wasn't my favourite outing because I'd rather go over to the park and play football or watch a game."

David's whole life was football. He played in the park, he played for his club, his school, his borough and his county. He watched his dad play Sunday football and afterwards begged him not to get changed and instead kick a ball about with him.

"My mum would be dead worried because it would be 11 o'clock at night and we still weren't home from one of Dad's Sunday league matches," Beckham once recalled. "but it was only because I hadn't practised my free kicks and corners enough. I used to beg him to stay on and be in goal for a few more."

The lad was obsessed, so it's not hard to imagine the excitement of December 1985 when, aged 10, he made his first-ever trip to Old Trafford. He'd seen the famous stadium on *Match of the Day* and dreamed of one day gracing its hallowed turf, so when Ted arranged an outing to see United play Tottenham David wasn't disappointed by the 0–0 scoreline and returned home with armfuls of United flags, scarves and t-shirts. He'd be out there on the pitch sooner than he thought.

Watching *Blue Peter* a few months later, David saw an item about a soccer skills competition organised by Bobby Charlton, one of the greatest players United and England have ever seen. Of course he entered. His Tottenham-supporting grandad Joseph forked out the £125 entry fee and, in what David later described as "the defining moment in my career", he won the London area competition and made it through to the final to be held at ... Old Trafford.

And so it was that on 7 December 1986 Beckham walked out at the aptly nicknamed "Theatre of Dreams" for the first time – only to be roundly booed! When the stadium announcer told Old Trafford he was from the Spurs hotbed of Chingford, the Tottenham fans in the ground started cheering. But when the announcer added he was a Man United fan they started booing and jeering just as David dribbled in front of them. Despite knocking over a couple of cones, it didn't put him seriously out of his stride and he went on to win the competition with the highest score ever recorded. Bobby Charlton told the crowd: "Here we have a destined star."

"As well as his ability with the ball, I recall the biggest thing that struck me was his determination to be a footballer," Charlton told the *Manchester Evening News* a few years later. "His desire to do

There was never any doubt about young David's ability, just his size. As his Ridgeway Rovers coach Steve Kirby put it, "He had legs like a canary."

well was very noticeable and he'd go anywhere to achieve his ambition."

Next stop the Nou Camp. David's prize for winning the skills competition was a trip to Barcelona. So, fresh-faced and spiky-haired, and complete with comedy sunglasses and TSB-sponsored t-shirt, Chingford's rising star was packed off for two weeks training with Barcelona's reserve and youth teams.

"It was a thrilling time, I walked around most of the time with my mouth gaping open," he says in his (first) autobiography *My Story*.

Having flown home in the middle of the trip to play for Ridgeway Rovers in a cup final, Beckham returned and was photographed with Barça players Gary Lineker and Mark Hughes and manager Terry Venables.

"Mr Venables gave me some advice then which I've never forgotten," Beckham said later. "He told me to practise, practise and keep on practising."

Not that he needed any prompting. During an appearance showing off his skills on daytime TV show *This Afternoon* following the Bobby Charlton competition win, presenter Sarah Kennedy asked if he had watched the year's big event, the Royal Wedding of Prince Andrew and Sarah Ferguson.

"No," replied Becks matter of factly, "I was in the park playing football."

By now Beckham was training twice a week with Spurs (in his United kit, of course) but his dream of becoming a professional footballer looked increasingly threatened by his lack of inches. He missed out on selection by England Schoolboys because of his size, despite getting down to the final 70 and having starred for Waltham Forest Boys and Essex Boys. It was a worrying time for the football-mad youngster, unprepared for anything other than playing the game he loved.

"I didn't like the classroom much," he admitted later. "Football was the only thing on my mind. I wasn't very interested in school so I can't remember much about the lessons, except for the art classes which I enjoyed."

Perhaps in preparation for the disappointment of not making it, Ted arranged for David to get his first taste of the "real world" when, aged 12, he took an evening job at Walthamstow Dog Track where he was paid £2 an hour to collect glasses and empty ashtrays. Ex-Wimbledon manager and greyhound racing fanatic Joe Kinnear claims to remember being served by him, and if it hadn't been for Malcolm Fidgeon he might still be there now.

Fidgeon, one of Manchester United's vast army of scouts, just happened to be at a match in Fairlop, Essex, between Waltham Forest Boys and Redbridge. David had no idea there was a United scout standing on the side of the pitch, but he ended up playing the game of his life. Unlike the Spurs and Arsenal scouts and coaches who had their doubts about Beckham's potential to make it as a pro footballer, Fidgeon saw beyond David's height and build and on the strength of that one game decided immediately to recommend him to United manager Alex Ferguson.

Fidgeon remembers the day well:

"Sometimes he got knocked off the ball because he wasn't big enough. But I was looking for a potential Manchester United footballer at 18 or 19, not 14. For his size David hit the ball very firmly but, more importantly, very accurately. He was very frail and tiny but he could do things the other boys couldn't and I thought he wouldn't disgrace himself if he was given the opportunity of a United trial."

Mum Sandra also remembers the day clearly as it was one of the few games dad Ted couldn't make. He was working.

"I stood outside waiting because David was always last out of the changing rooms," recalls Sandra. "When he finally emerged I said, 'It's a good job you had a good game'. 'Why's that?' he said and I replied: 'The Manchester United scout was there and he's coming round to see us tonight'. He jumped in the air and cried because he always used to say: 'I don't think they're going to find me down here'."

It's a running joke in the Beckham household, who was more nervous about David's trials with United – David or Ted? This was the fruition of two people's dreams. The payback for all those hours spent in the park. For Beckham this series of trials meant everything, and he'd wait with his nose pressed up against the window for Fidgeon to arrive at 8 o'clock in the morning and whisk him up the M6 to Manchester whenever he had one.

Young David surveys the scene at Barcelona's magnificent Camp Nou where, 12 years later, he would enjoy his greatest moment in a Manchester United shirt.

"My mum tells me that I stood at the front window and if it got to five past eight I'd start to get really nervous and wonder if he was ever going to come," says Beckham in *My Story*. "Then I would see his car, dash upstairs, grab my kit from the top of the bed, say a quick 'bye' over my shoulder and off we went up the motorway. Those were brilliant days."

Fidgeon recalls: "As we travelled together from Essex he never showed his emotions much but I could see he was excited and there was a touch of steel about him."

The scout remembers that the young Cockney Red made a good impression in those first trials. "He did well and Alex Ferguson was very helpful," says Fidgeon. "He makes every boy feel part of things in an informal way, calling out things like 'Hey Beckham, when are you going to grow a bit?'."

Whatever their differences now, it was this personal touch from the United manager which most impressed the young Beckham about the set-up at the club's old training ground at The Cliff. At the time he was still being courted by Spurs, then managed by former Barcelona boss Terry Venables. But since that first meeting at the Nou Camp, Venables had gone down in young David's estimation.

"I think I met Terry Venables once in two years at Tottenham," said Beckham many years later. "That doesn't exactly inspire you to join a club". Apparently Venables asked him if he'd be interested in signing for Spurs whilst grappling under the table for a bag of crisps he'd dropped. But in truth even if Venables had been looking him squarely in the eye and offering him a lifetime supply of cheese and onion, there was only one club David was ever going to play for.

David Beckham signed trainee forms with Manchester United in a restaurant on the outskirts of Manchester on his 14th birthday. The whole Beckham family and Malcolm Fidgeon making the trip, getting stuck in traffic and keeping United boss Alex Ferguson waiting on his own for two hours with just a contract and a birthday cake for company. Ferguson suspected it would be worth the wait.

After that David spent as much time as he could at Old Trafford, including the entire summer holidays when he would stay at halls of residence with 30 other young hopefuls and train at The Cliff every day.

"When I first arrived at United it was a bit scary," he admits in *My World*, "partly because all my heroes were from United. I had their pictures on my bedroom wall … especially Bryan Robson – I had a shirt with his name on."

During term time, whenever United played in London Ted, Sandra and David would be special guests of the club. He was even the team's mascot for one game with West Ham, running out in United kit with the team for the pre-match warm-up.

"Afterwards I managed to sneak my way into the row behind the United bench to watch the game," he recalled later. "When Clayton Blackmore was brought on and the TV cameras showed a close-up of the substitution, there was this young kid with spiky hair right in the picture. My first TV exposure, standing right behind Alex Ferguson as he shouted out his instructions. Even then I couldn't get enough of United. I knew it was the club for me."

Former United defender turned Birmingham boss Steve Bruce remembers: "Every time we went to London he was there. One day in the dressing room at the League Cup Final he was picking up the boots and putting them in the skip just to be involved. We knew at the time this kid must be a bit special, just from the treatment he was getting."

Not even the temptations of youth could distract young David from his ultimate goal:

"On a Saturday night my friends would be on the corner of the street with a bottle of Woodpecker and a fag or going to house parties, but I'd be watching *Match of the Day* and going to bed early because I had a game in the morning."

The dedication was there for all to see, and at the age of 16 David Beckham's dream came true when he was offered a trainee contract with United. It would mean £29.50 plus £10 expenses per week. It would also mean moving to Manchester, away from his close-knit family. It was a big decision, but not a tough one. He'd have gladly walked to Old Trafford in his bare feet and his dad would probably have shoved him out of the front door to do it. It didn't come to that, of course, and on 8 July 1991 David Beckham signed for Manchester United.

Pages 16/17: David and his Ridgeway Rovers teammates.
Left: Seeing the world through very, very large sunglasses!

growing **pains**

David's dream of signing for Manchester United had come true. He was a United player, a pro footballer. He'd made it, right? Wrong.

Having left the bosom of the close-knit Beckham family home aged just 16, David found himself in a strange new world. Miles away from his mum, dad and his two sisters Lynne and Joanne, and suddenly separated from his mates who he'd played football with since he could remember, he was on his own, and he found it tough.

He was kicked out of his digs twice in the first few weeks, once through no fault of his own when another player was caught taking food from the kitchen without permission, the second time for complaining about the food. And at The Cliff, Manchester United's famous old training ground, he suddenly found himself surrounded by the best young players in the country who were not only as good as him or better, they were bigger and stronger.

Beckham could handle that. He'd been playing against bigger players all his life, even turning out for his dad's Sunday League team when he was only 14. He knew how to look after himself, but there were other problems. With his cockney accent and London clothes, Beckham stood out from the other trainees battling for a future in the game.

"A lot of the local lads didn't like me when I first came," he later admitted.

Beckham was also in awe of the seasoned pros all around. Men like Bryan Robson, Steve Bruce and Mark Hughes, big-name stars who not so long ago had been plastered over David's bedroom walls, now were all around him.

"It can be quite difficult coming to a club with players of international pedigree," he said. "It's even more difficult when you're a fan and you feel like getting your autograph book out."

David had some serious growing up to do, in more ways than one. He was still slight for his age and as soon as he arrived at United full-time he was put on a strict diet and weight-training programme.

While a less determined character might have slipped into more traditional teenage pursuits, David's obsession with playing football for Manchester United never waned.

"He was very clean living," says Malcolm Fidgeon, who kept tabs on the prodigy he'd spotted. "He would be in bed by 9pm and was never distracted by the pull of pubs and clubs."

However much David wanted to fit in, he never strayed off his chosen path. On one rare night out to a pizza restaurant with team-mates, David remembers being mocked for ordering a glass of milk instead of beer.

And gradually he settled in at United. At first he was used sparingly in the "B" youth team, the club monitoring the progress of his weight training and giving him time to settle in. Off the pitch he'd been found new digs run by Annie and Tommy Kay (he was proud to be given a room once occupied by United legend Mark Hughes).

"When David moved in I was under pressure to make him comfortable," Annie Kay recalled years later. "The club told me he was an amazing prospect they didn't want to lose. At first he was homesick, but he was a joy to look after, easily the tidiest player I have ever had – shoes lined up, shirts on hangers."

The feeling was mutual. "It was like having another mum and dad," David explains in *My World*. "I was with them for two and a half years and they made me feel at home and settled, so I could really concentrate on my football."

Well, not just football. "David always liked his

clothes," added Annie Kay, "When he arrived he had so many clothes that there was no wardrobe space left for the other lad who was staying with us. He was always trying outfits on and saying: 'What do you think of this one Annie?'."

And Beckham was starting to look as good on the pitch as he was off it, too. After just 14 starts for the "B" team in his first season at Old Trafford, towards the end of the campaign Beckham found himself fast-tracked into the "A" team, a side the legendary United youth coach Eric Harrison refers to as "the greatest youth team ever". Featuring the likes of Gary Neville, Ryan Giggs and Nicky Butt, the team had already reached the semi-final of the FA Youth Cup when Beckham was called up for the second leg against Spurs at White Hart Lane. He played well, keeping his place in central midfield alongside Butt and scoring in the final against Crystal Palace. It was the first time United had won the competition since 1964.

Beckham impressed United's coaches with his skill but even more with his attitude. Eric Harrison and his team couldn't get rid of him. He came in for extra training every day, practising free-kicks until it was dark as if he was back at Chase Lane Park.

"In youth team matches, if we got a free-kick 25 yards from goal, I used to be disappointed if he didn't score," recalls Harrison. "That was because I saw him practising them in training. He came back voluntarily when I took the Under-16s after school, his third training session of the day."

A week short of his 17th birthday, Beckham was called up to play for the reserves against Leeds. Then on 23 September 1992, at the start of his second season at Old Trafford with the club in the midst of a midfield injury crisis, he was selected for the first team squad for a league cup tie away at Brighton & Hove Albion.

"It was a night match and I remember sitting on the bench terrified that I might get on," he said later. "Next thing I know I have taken Andrei Kanchelskis's place. I've still got the shirt."

The game ended 1–1, but it had been 1–0 when David had come on in the 71st minute and his elation at making his debut was soon blown away by first taste of Fergie's famous "hairdryer treatment".

"I got a bit of a mouthful at the end…" he says in *My Story*. "… I think the gist of his message was, 'You're in the big time now, son, this is what it's all about'."

Fergie's verbal volley was nothing compared to the events of the next 18 months. Little did he know that his debut would be his only taste of first-team action for well over a year. The problem was not a new one. He might not have "canary legs" any more, but David was still behind most of his peers when it came to the physical side of the game.

Eric Harrison recalls: "David had to be nursed along a bit between the ages of 16 and 17 because his physique was changing dramatically. He literally shot up in size. The stamina was still there, but the strength was not."

While his youth team pals like Nicky Butt, Gary Neville and even Paul Scholes advanced rapidly into the first-team frame, Beckham only played four games for the reserves in 1992/93 as Harrison preferred to let him develop his strength in the youth team. He scored 12 league goals in 25 matches, the side once again reaching the FA Youth Cup Final but losing to Leeds. Harrison remembers several heart-to-heart chats with young Beckham when he urged him to be patient. "Your time will come," he said. By the start of the 1993/94 season this softly softly approach looked to be paying off.

"Quickly he had been transformed from a small, skinny kid to a six-footer with broad shoulders," says Harrison. "We now had a midfield player who had all the skill in the world, could run for fun and had the physique to go with it."

1993/94 was the season when Fergie unleashed his fledglings, sending a ludicrously inexperienced "reserve" team to defeat Port Vale 2–1 in the Coca Cola Cup in October 1994.

The following day the *Today* newspaper's reporter gushed: "David Beckham has vision and an incredible passing ability that United often lack, even in their awesome first-team line-up".

In the following round young United were beaten 2–0 away at Newcastle, but it was David's first-ever appearance in the famous number 7 shirt.

Then on 7 December, with United massively handicapped by UEFA's "four foreigners" rule and all but out of the Champions League, Alex Ferguson decided to blood some of his prized youngsters in the final group match against Galatasaray. David not only realised his dream of starting for United at Old Trafford, but in the 37th minute he also powered in United's second goal in a 4–0 win.

"After the goal the first thing I remember is Eric coming towards me," says Beckham. "We met in mid-air as I jumped to celebrate. My mum was in tears and when I scored my dad shot out of his seat and accidentally head-butted the bloke next to him."

Beckham had taken his big chance with both hands. The famously aloof Eric Cantona had acknowledged him. He felt like a first-team player now and he was starting to live like one. He was still living in digs with the Kays but, having passed his driving test first time, he bought a modest Ford Escort, the first in a long line of motors. Then after completing his apprenticeship, David splashed out on a new Golf.

He was living the dream, alright, but unlike his new VW, his career continued to splutter. The feeling within the club was that despite promising signs he still wasn't ready.

"We all knew that David had great ability, but people said he was a bit soft going into tackles and headers," explains Gary Neville.

Beckham was 19. At his age Ryan Giggs had been a first-team regular for two years, and his youth team pals Neville, Butt and Scholes had all leapfrogged him in the first-team pecking order. So when Alex Ferguson called him into his office in March 1995, four months and not a single first team appearance since Galatasaray later, to tell him he was sending him out on loan to Third Division Preston North End, Beckham thought his United dream was over.

"I was shocked at first, then a little hurt that he should want to let me go," he recalls in *My Story*. "Then I was downright worried about it. What if United didn't fancy me any more?"

Ferguson explained to his worried player that he wanted to him to toughen up in the rough and tumble of Division Three.

Gary Peters was Preston's manager at the time. "Alex believed the only ingredient missing from David's game was the physical aspect," he says. "So

when I asked Alex about taking one of his players on loan he couldn't believe I wanted Beckham. But I'd watched him in youth and reserve team games and been impressed. I was a bit worried that David would struggle with the physical side though. I had to bully and cajole him a bit, but David soon got the message he had to mix it with the hard nuts – and he learned quickly."

He was learning lessons off the pitch too.

"At United, you get used to having the best of everything," he said afterwards. "When I turned up at Preston on the first day I didn't have any kit with me and I bet the players thought I was a right flash sod. But after the first game, I think they realised I was there to work."

And take the free-kicks, of course. David recalls being hauled into the centre circle on his first day, in front of the whole Preston squad:

"Gary Peters said, 'Right, this fella's going to take all the free-kicks and corners because he's much better at it than you lot'. I didn't know where to look."

Peters was right though. In his first match David came on as a sub and scored direct from a corner, a 2–2 draw against Doncaster.

"It was no fluke," enthuses Peters. "Then he scored with a free-kick against Fulham that was pure class. The fans loved him."

After five games Alex Ferguson was on the phone to an unsurprised Gary Peters to ask for his player back. David returned to United, despite Preston's supporters begging the club to abandon plans for a new £4 million stand and put in a bid for him.

"That month at Preston turned my whole career around," he says now. "I needed to be encouraged, and Preston did that for me. I was almost disappointed to get called back after five games."

Not for long. Having played for Preston against Lincoln the previous Saturday in front of a crowd of 5,487, on 2 April he made his United league debut against Leeds in front of 43,000 at Old Trafford. The game ended in a 0–0 draw and United ended the season empty-handed after losing their league title to Blackburn Rovers and the FA Cup Final to Everton. But Beckham had proved he could handle the physical and mental pressures of first-team football. He was ready.

Beckham realises he's got this football malarkey licked!

winning
the
double
with
kids

With the benefit of hindsight, it's a ridiculous thing to say. *Match of the Day* pundit Alan Hansen sits back with confidence bordering on arrogance that made him such a great player and delivers the line that will haunt him forever. "You can't win anything with kids," he declares, the BBC smugness oozing from every pore.

To be fair on Hansen, from the outside it did look like Ferguson had just committed football suicide. It was the first day of the 1995/96 season, and Manchester United had been tonked 3–1 by Aston Villa. Having ended the previous season trophyless, the United manager had ditched three of his biggest name at the club – Paul Ince, Andrei Kanchelskis and Mark Hughes – and replaced them with a bunch of youth teamers with a mere handful of first-team games behind him.

Even die-hard United fans were running scared. A poll in the *Manchester Evening News* indicated a staggering 53 per cent of them believed their legendary gaffer had lost it and they wanted him out. Even if many who phoned up were mischievous Man City fans, the feeling in football was that with the team's inspiration, Eric Cantona, banned until October the Manchester United winning machine had gone seriously off the rails.

And as the *Match of the Day* team picked holes in United's opening day performance at Villa Park, predicting grey clouds over Old Trafford as gloomy as the club's dodgy new away kit, one incident in the match received just passing attention. That was the moment when, with his team 3–0 down, substitute David Beckham – playing in the number 24 shirt – rocketted an unstoppable shot into the top corner of the Aston Villa net. Beckham had come off the bench to replace Phil Neville, and it would be a while before he was back on it.

For this was to be the season where Beckham, along with the nucleus of that '92 FA Youth Cup-winning team, set the Premiership on fire with their fresh-faced flair and exuberance. Hours and hours in the gym and the loan spell at Preston had given Beckham the brawn to match his footballing brain, now he was ready to fulfil the potential first identified in him by his dad all those years ago.

Yet, amazingly, during the summer of 1995 Beckham had feared it was the same old story with his stop/start United career. He was 20, he'd still only ever started one league game and according to the papers he didn't even know if United were going to offer him a new contract. Arsenal and Spurs were sniffing round, so unlike his former youth team peers Beckham appointed an agent (Tony Stephens, who also advised Alan Shearer) which apparently displeased Ferguson and United. In one story in the *Manchester Evening News* he was branded a "rebel".

In fact like the rest of the young United stars Beckham eagerly signed a four year deal worth what now seems a paltry £2,000 a week plus a £20,000 signing-on fee. Stephens had only been hired in an advisory capacity, Beckham insisted and, giving an early insight into the priorities of his young player Alex Ferguson told the press: "The only slight difficulty we had [with his contract] was over whether he would get a club car or not. But that was sorted out. He'll get one after so many matches."

And the matches soon started added up. Ferguson had seen enough to tell him the kids were ready, and within weeks of the Villa defeat the media would be waxing lyrical about United's young team. World famous for the Busby Babes team of the fifties, forty years on United had Fergie's Fledglings.

Alongside Gary Neville, Scholes and Butt, Beckham started the next game at home to West

"Here you go son. I've been practising this since I was your height!"

28

Ham. They won 2–1. He kept his place for the win over Wimbledon at Old Trafford the following week and for the next five games, all of which the new-look United emerged from victorious. The youngsters even got a mention in the "comment" column in *The Sun*, under the headline, "Who needs big name stars?".

And despite United dropping their first points of the season since the Villa Park defeat in a 0-0 draw away to Sheffield Wednesday, the *Daily Telegraph*'s Henry Winter afterwards enthused about the team's performance, identifying Beckham as the "pick of the crop" of United's youngsters: "His composure is breathtaking, as is his vision. United's strong last 20 minutes had much to do with his move to central midfield…" Though, perceptively, Winter added the caveat: "…however, it also led to Wednesday's best chances. With Butt tiring after a midweek virus and Beckham more of a creator than destroyer, Beckham's central midfield was exposed."

As a young player Beckham had always thrived in central midfield. It was where he loved to play, bossing the game from the middle of the park, spraying balls all over the pitch and getting forward and into shooting range. But in the 500-mile-an-hour pace of your average Premiership match Ferguson realised he was far more effective out on the right, staying out of trouble and firing in his pin-point crossfield passes and crosses. With the likes of Keane and Butt to hold the team together in the middle, Ferguson always believed Beckham would be more effective staying out wide.

In his first ever interview with *Manchester United* magazine – complete with his first ever moody photoshoot – Beckham revealed he didn't agree. "I do think central midfield is my best position. But it's an honour to play for this club, I'd play anywhere for United… although I'm not sure how Peter [Schmeichel] would react if I put gloves on."

Effectively Beckham and Fergie agreed to disagree and, however good-natured, it was to be their first public disagreement. Not exactly a portent of what was to come, perhaps, but an indication that despite his shyness in interviews, for a twenty-year-old kid Beckham had a striking inner self-confidence – a confidence that was having an

influence on his life off the pitch, as well as on it. For while team-mates like Paul Scholes and Nicky Butt shunned the limelight, Beckham thrived as the centre of attention – a fact not lost on *United* magazine editor Rachel Jervis when she attended Beckham's early photo sessions.

"When he first broke into the first team he was shy and found interviews hard," she remembers, "but the camera always loved him. If we did a shoot with him, we had to lock the mag in the office because everyone wanted to see the pictures straight away."

Some of Beckham's admirers, it seemed, did not want to talk about the merits of a diamond midfield or the peculiarities of the offside trap. Despite former teacher John Bullock telling a newspaper, "if you stuck a girl or a ball in front of David, he'd pick up the ball," for the first time Beckham began showing an interest in the opposite sex. He briefly dated blonde air stewardess Lisa Rys-Halska, before making his first appearance in the gossip columns when the *Manchester Evening News* revealed his romance with part-time model Julie Killelea. It didn't last (Julie is now married to Phil Neville) and some of David's early girlfriends complained of a lack of commitment on his part.

In his colourful analysis *Posh n Becks*, royal biographer Andrew Morton insists: "He gave the impression that he would rather be making passes on the soccer pitch than in the bedroom." And according to Morton one model he dated, Leoni Mazell, said that during their brief relationship Beckham only came alive when talking about football to her father while another, Miss UK Anna Bartley, claimed, "He took me to a restaurant but said almost nothing."

Having spent his entire childhood and teenage years focused only on becoming a footballer Beckham was dipping his toe into the waters of real life, but football remained priority number one. And despite buying a house two doors down from the more gregarious Ryan Giggs and socialising with his new neighbour and his mates, he rarely drank alcohol and would spend most nights tucked up at home with a Stephen King book or listening to rap music. Most unusually for a twenty-something, he was also obsessed with tidiness and apparently spent hours neatly folding his new designer clothes and cleaning his latest fast car.

Back at United Beckham's flashy image made him the butt of friendly dressing room humour, most notably from team joker David May, but not everyone gave him such an easy ride. He might not have been the skinny kid of a couple of years back, but on the pitch he was still a pretty boy compared to most of the Premiership's hardened veterans. "I lacked size and a physical presence then," admits Beckham in *My World*, going on to tell an anecdote of Nottingham Forest's Stuart Pearce "whacking me right up into the air and leaving me in a heap on the grass."

But this kind of treatment didn't faze Beckham. He gave as good as he got, in fact, picking up 21 disciplinary points before Christmas. Not only was he used to playing against bigger players who would try to compensate for the difference in skill by illegal means, he was playing brilliantly for Manchester United and he wasn't giving up his place for anyone. Well, except perhaps a certain Eric Cantona.

The return of United's inspirational captain from his suspension for attacking a Crystal Palace supporter in a match during the previous season saw Beckham left out of the starting eleven for the first time since the first game of the season. But Ferguson made a point of telling the press his young star was not being dropped, merely rested. And if Beckham had to make way for anyone, no doubt he would have chosen the Frenchman. Like most of the players at United he was in awe of the great man, and recalls a glance of acknowledgement or nod of approval from Cantona would have him walking on cloud nine for the rest of the day.

The Frenchman clearly had a lot of time for Beckham too, inviting the young player to do extra training with him at The Cliff.

"For most of the time it involved crossing the ball for him," enthuses Beckham in *My Story*, "and I believe the fact that I am considered such a good crosser now is that I was so desperate to get it right for him. Eric stood for perfection. He showed that you shouldn't be content with second best."

If Beckham's season had been spectacular so far,

as United's league and cup campaigns reached their climax it was about to go into orbit. A two-goal blast in the crunch 5–0 league thrashing of Nottingham Forest at Old Trafford set the scene, but it was his performance in the FA Cup semi-final which truly imprinted his name on the nation's consciousness.

With the score locked at 1-1 in the Villa Park clash with Chelsea, Beckham smartly collected a mis-hit backpass, cut in and angled towards goal with the 50,000 crowd and the watching millions holding their breath. Holding off the Chelsea defence he steadied himself, and calmly sidefooted the ball into the back of the net. The twenty-year-old United fan and first team newcomer had just fired Manchester United into the FA Cup Final.

"I can't describe the feeling I got when I scored," he said later of the goal, "I have never felt anything like that."

A hundred and fifty miles or so away, Val Yerall, a Walthamstow dog track employee was enjoying a relaxing Sunday afternoon. "You could have knocked me down with a feather duster when I was watching the box and there he was, knocking in the winner for Manchester United in a cup semi-final," she told the *Daily Mirror*. "I thought, 'I know that face. Didn't he used to collect the empties?'."

Now Beckham's cup was overflowing. At the end of just his 34th league appearance on 5 May, (three days after his 21st birthday) he picked up his first senior trophy, when a 3–0 win against Middlesbrough gave United the Premier League trophy. Six days later he ran out at Wembley for the FA Cup Final, literally bringing a tear to his dad's eye and helping United to a 1–0 win over Liverpool making them the first team ever to win the league and FA Cup Double twice. If his career had ended at the final whistle on that Wembley afternoon he could have retired fulfilled – in one season he'd lived virtually every dream a football-crazy kid could ever think up.

"For me it is still unbelievable playing at a club you have watched all your life," he admitted. "I pinch myself in training when I look around and see all the great players I mix with, it's amazing."

Amazing, perhaps, but for David Beckham and his ability to perform miracles with a football more powerful adjectives would soon be required.

the
wonder
years

With the ball at his feet, David Beckham glanced up and saw Wimbledon goalkeeper Neil Sullivan off his line. Having landed the coveted United number 10 shirt, starred in the Charity Shield and been tipped for an England call-up, Beckham and his team were 2–0 up on the opening day of the season. A young footballer's life couldn't get much better. But 57 yards from goal and still inside his own half, David Beckham was about to make the decision that would change his forever.

Instead of passing it short or moving down the line to play out time, Beckham lowered his head, took aim and swept his right boot through the ball. It sailed into the air and Selhurst Park went eerily silent. A few seconds later the place, packed with United fans, erupted. Sullivan had scrambled back but the ball had sailed over his head and into the back of the net. Beckham raised his arms and turned to the crowd but in truth he could have had no idea what he'd just done.

The next day, Beckham's image was plastered all over the front and back pages of virtually every newspaper. The *Daily Mirror* called it a "Wonder Goal", the *News of the World* insisted: "There is no argument David Beckham's unbelievable strike will be the goal of the season. The only debate is whether it is the greatest goal ever."

Eric Cantona reckoned so, describing it as "the best goal I have ever seen". Alex Ferguson compared it to Pele's long-ranger against Czechoslovakia in the 1970 World Cup – except the greatest footballer of all time missed!

Beckham was typically matter of fact, explaining in *My Story*: "I swept the ball in the air and it seemed to hang there for ages. My dad, who was behind the goal, said he was watching it go up when the bloke in front stood up and he didn't see it land

in the back of the net. I thought it would be close because I'd hit it perfectly. On the bench, Alex Ferguson said he was muttering, 'Oh, trust him.' A couple of seconds later I was celebrating one of the most incredible moments of my career."

The recollections of David's dad are more revealing, Ted insisting that his son was more excited by Eric Cantona coming up to him in the changing room afterwards and congratulating him with the words, "Beautiful goal, David".

From that moment on Beckham, like Cantona, was different. No longer just one member of a group of exceptionally talented young United players, he was David Beckham, scorer of the wonder goal from inside his own half. Newspapers began tracking down his old teachers and school-mates for quotes and tales of similar long-distance goals for Ridgeway Rovers, interview requests quadrupled and even people with no interest in 22 people kicking a ball about knew his name.

Four days after his Selhurst Park stunner, English football's new hope was called into the England squad by new manager Glenn Hoddle. He would have been called up even if his Selhurst Park shot had soared over the bar and into the Sainsbury's car park next door. For while Venables' England had taken the nation to the brink of glory at Euro '96 the previous summer, Beckham had been starring for England Under-21s at the Toulon tournament in France under the watchful eye of boss Graham Rix. Rix told Hoddle Beckham was ready:

"You can look at players of that age and tell the ones who will fail, who will make it and those who will be stars," he said. "Becks is going to be a true star. Everybody knows what he can do with the ball at his feet, but that's not as important as what goes on away from game situations. Tell him something in

Beckham gives United's hat-trick hero Andrew Cole a congratulatory smacker during United's 3–1 Champions League win away to Feyenoord, 5 November 1997.

training and it's done instantly, ask him to do something and there's no moans, raised eyebrows or questions, he just gets on with it. He's still learning his trade, but give him five years and I think Alex Ferguson will regard him as his general."

21-year-old Beckham made his international debut the following week in England's first World Cup qualifier for France '98, a 3–0 win over Moldova. He acquitted himself well as an attacking wing back in a five-man defence, and after the game asked manager Glenn Hoddle to sign his shirt.

Back at United he was ever-present in the team despite the recent signings of Czech Euro '96 star Karel Poborsky and Jordi Cruyff from Barcelona, both of whom had been expected to stake a claim on the right side of midfield. It was a whirlwind. Suddenly from being a prospect for the future Beckham was England's hottest young talent. Boot manufacturers Adidas stepped in to offer him £200,000 a year to wear their new Predator boots.

Amazingly, Beckham had borrowed a pair of the new boots and was wearing them when he scored his 57-yarder against Wimbledon. The story was a marketing dream and within months Adidas had increased his £800,000 deal to £4 million by giving him cash for every pair of Predators sold.

United were also quick to acknowledge Beckham's spiralling potential not just a player but as a means of selling anything from replica shirts to duvet covers and coffee cups moulded into the shape of his head. In October 1996 he signed a brand new five-year contract worth £1.5 million which put him on a par with the club's established stars.

"I'd sign for life if I had the chance," he said.

And at an Adidas press conference where he was pictured with an armful of his new boots he insisted: "I don't think of myself as a superstar. I've been in the papers quite a bit, but I'm taking it in my stride."

Certainly, his new-found fame was not diminishing Beckham's performances for United. He scored the winner against old rivals Liverpool with another stunning strike and by the end of October only Eric Cantona had racked up more than his 1,334 minutes on the pitch. He had also cemented his place in the England team alongside his great friend Gary Neville, and it was in the company of his United

team-mate in the unlikely setting of Tiblisi, Georgia, that Beckham's life took its next dramatic turn.

Whiling away the boredom between training sessions on the eve of an England World Cup qualifier, the pair were watching MTV in their shared hotel room when the new Spice Girls video came on. This was at the height of Girl Power and the video for the song *Say You'll Be There* featured Posh Spice in a skin-tight black latex cat-suit complete with six-inch stilletos and dominatrix whip. Beckham was transfixed, and apparently turned to Gary and said: "That's the girl for me, and I'm going to get her".

It's a corny story, but it gets worse. Back home in England at about the same time, journalist Juliette Wills interviewed the Spice Girls for a football magazine. A tough assignment, as none of them, not even Sporty, knew much about football. So to get things going she produced a series of pictures of footballers and asked them all to pick their favourite. According to Wills, Posh picked out David and said, "Wow he's gorgeous, how can I meet him?" and refused to give the picture back.

How much of all these anecdotes are true and how much is apocryphal we'll never know, but what is certain is that on 22 February 1997 Posh Spice, real name Victoria Adams, found herself in the players' bar at Stamford Bridge after United had drawn 1–1 with Chelsea. With her long-term boyfriend Stuart Bilton conveniently laid up in hospital after a serious skiing accident, Beckham spotted her across the crowded room and their eyes met. Unfortunately the young footballer, overcome by shyness, was unable to capitalise on this romantic opportunity and instead could muster nothing more than a comical wave before turning away embarrassed.

"I couldn't believe that I'd wasted my big chance," he said later.

He was to get another one, but he nearly blew that too. Three weeks later Posh and Sporty Spice turned up at Old Trafford to watch United play Sheffield Wednesday. They were paraded on the pitch at half-time and ended up in the players' lounge again. After the game the love-struck pair's paths crossed at the bar, their eyes met again. This time Beckham could only stutter "Hello", before walking away shyly.

"She was convinced at this point that I didn't want to know her," David recalls in *My World*, "but the truth is I was very shy. Luckily she'd had a couple of glasses of wine, so she had the courage to come over and we started talking. I felt so self-conscious, because I could see everyone was watching us, but soon we were chatting away. By the end we were the only ones left in the lounge. Finally, Victoria turned round and said something like, 'So, are you going to give me your number?'."

Beckham refused, insisting she give him hers instead, writing it down on seven scraps of paper which he left all round his house so he didn't lose it. And so it began. The next day David drove to London after training at The Cliff and they went round to visit fellow Spice Girl Mel C. Victoria remembers that whenever she stood up to leave the room he would stand up too.

"At first I thought there was something wrong," she said. "Then I realised he was just being polite. I never had anyone treat me like that."

They went to the cinema to see *Jerry Maguire* and he nervously put his hand on her knee ("I pretended I'd done it by accident"). He bought her a Prada handbag, she bought him an enormous fluffy bunny, they were like a pair of besotted teenagers. And though they tried to keep their relationship a secret, soon pictures of the couple on shopping sprees, coming out of restaurants, snogging in the street were all over the papers.

For the tabloids it was too good to be true. The hottest young footballer in England gets it on with a member of the biggest girl band in history. It was the kind of dream ticket that management teams and PR companies dream of, yet this was no set-up. Victoria is said to have slept in one of David's old England shirts whenever they were apart, and they spent hours and hours on the phone to each other. Andrew Morton claims if David was in a restaurant without her he'd phone her to discuss what to order, and in one interview Beckham admitted that his mobile phone bill was £2,000 a month.

There's no doubt Sir Alex Ferguson feared the showbiz lifestyle that his hottest prospect had slipped so quickly into would affect his football at a crucial stage of its development. If Fergie had his way his young players would be married to nice quiet girls from an early age, spending their afternoons after training resting at home. Beckham was pelting up and down the motorway between London and Manchester, being pictured at movie premieres and in the street weighed down with bags full of designer clothes.

But as long as he was never late for training, didn't break club rules and continued to perform on the pitch, there was little Fergie could do. And anyway Beckham was the club's highest scoring midfielder as United surged to their fourth championship win in five years and reached the semi-finals of the European Cup. His form wasn't suffering, it was soaring, and he picked up the PFA Young Player of the Year Award, United's Player of the Season Award and later on even the BBC1's Young Sports Personality award. With a little help from his floppy locks he was even named as the new Brylcreem boy, earning himself a slick £1 million in the process.

Fame and fortune off the pitch seemed to be having the opposite effect to that which Fergie feared, actually giving Beckham confidence on it.

But by the summer of 1997 it was getting ridiculous. In August the *Manchester Evening News* reported that David Beckham had visited his local supermarket and bought a lettuce and some cherries.

"When he handed over £8 worth of cherries I thought, 'I hope your Mum doesn't tell you off for spending so much'," noted the check-out girl at the centre of this stunning world exclusive.

At first David and Victoria had played up to the cameras, posing when they spotted the paparazzi and seeing the funny side. They were young and in love. But by the time Manchester United's official magazine interviewed Beckham on the day he was listed as Britain's 17th highest paid sportsman on £1.35 million a year, life in the proverbial goldfish bowl was becoming less of an attractive proposition.

"I'm sick of all the attention to be honest," he said. "I still enjoy being noticed by little kids and United fans, but I can't understand the fascination there is to know about everything I do. David Beckham was in a restaurant, David Beckham was on his mobile phone... I think it's out of order.

"Whenever I'm with Victoria we get followed. For

about a week a man on a motorbike followed me all the time. He was outside my house first thing in the morning and last thing at night. It started to get a bit worrying so I had to call the police.

"I want to be known for my football, nothing else," he added.

Beckham also started to receive threats from rival teams' supporters, hiring one of United's bodyguards to shadow him in public. He is said to have been a nervous wreck before matches when Victoria was coming to watch, unable to relax until he knew she was safely in her seat. For despite their busy lives, the couple were now inseparable and Beckham would drive, or even charter a plane, to be with her whenever United's players had a day off.

United's manager was becoming increasingly concerned. Despite handing Beckham the famous United number 7 shirt following the retirement of Eric Cantona, Ferguson left his young star on the bench for the Charity Shield and left him there for the first two matches of the 1997/98 Premiership season. Beckham had played for England in Le Tournoi (a pre-World Cup tournament) during the summer, getting himself needlessly booked twice and missing the final against Brazil.

Was the strain starting to show?

At a match against West Ham in September he was subjected relentlessly to an obscene chant about him and his girlfriend. So shocking was the level of abuse that match referee David Elleray felt compelled to ask Beckham if he was okay, and when United scored he went beserk, screaming back at his tormentors, his face contorted with rage.

Predictably, the song was soon reverberating around every stadium where United played.

"It's horrible," admitted Victoria. "I get depressed like everybody else. I try not to let it upset me, but I'm human. David just has to take it and get on with playing – it's so hard for him."

By now the world really was Posh and Becks crazy. When Becks splashed out on a brand new £70,000 Porsche it was front-page news. When he went to the cinema wearing glasses, vision experts were called in to pass comment. Rumours that the couple had secretly married were denied by the world's top legal brains.

For a 22-year-old man who had lived a relatively sheltered life, it must have bewildering, and one glance at the career paths of men like George Best and Paul Gascoigne gives an indication of the direction David Beckham's life might have gone in. And yet under all this scrutiny, with photographers literally tracking his every step, the world's media pouncing on every word, there was not one "boozy nightclub incident" or "kiss-and-tell shocker". Beyond the fast cars, diamond-encrusted jewellery and Gucci bags Posh and Becks were just an ordinary couple from Essex who hit the jackpot. They had won the lottery of life, yet claimed to be at their happiest curled up on the sofa with a takeaway watching *Friends*.

On 24 January 1998 David went down on one knee on a winter break to St Tropez and asked Victoria to marry him. The engagement was announced a few days later with a predictable frenzy of headlines. But despite all the hype, the really extraordinary part of David Beckham's life was still taking place on the football pitch every Saturday afternoon at 3 o' clock.

The highlight of the 1997/98 season for Beckham, however, was wearing the white of England not the red of United. For while his club were to discover just how much Arsene Wenger had transformed Arsenal by leading them to a sensational league and cup Double, England had uncovered the key to its footballing future. The only player to play in every World Cup qualifier for Glenn Hoddle's team, in October 1997 Beckham had been part of the midfield hub which held Italy to a famous 0–0 draw in the final match of Group Two. It was the first time Italy had ever failed to win in Rome and sent England to the 1998 World Cup in France.

"David has the potential to be a major star for his country for the next 10 years," said Hoddle.

In two mad years Beckham had gone from United hopeful to a £15,000 a week, multi-sponsored celebrity. Even his team-mates in the England squad nicknamed him "superstar".

"I'm only 22. Everything has come so fast it frightens me," Beckham said in an interview just before setting off to join up with the England squad.

He was right to be afraid.

Pages 38/39: The 57-yard wonder goal v Wimbledon. 17 August 1996.
Right: A PR agent's dream couple... but David and Victoria's love was genuine.

public
enemy
number
one

An Adidas billboard, featuring Beckham's face, which appeared all over the country early on 30 June 1998, proclaimed "After tonight, England v Argentina will be remembered for what an Englishman did with his feet."

Well, they got that right. The moment when Beckham instinctively flicked a petulant Predator at the calf of his Argentinian tormentor Diego Simeone is indelibly etched in the consciousness of English football. Gary Neville was not alone when, even before Danish referee Kim Milton Nielsen had whipped the red card from his pocket, he exclaimed: "What did you do that for?"

David Beckham's rise to the dizzy heights of fame and fortune was rapid enough, but his fall from grace was completed in an instant. By the time Simeone had fallen back clutching his calf in mock agony, Beckham's dream world was already collapsing around him. One split-second error of judgement was all it took to transform England's golden boy into such a figure of tabloid-fuelled hate that it's a miracle this isn't where the David Beckham story ends.

Even before his moment of madness, the 1998 World Cup had begun badly for Beckham. With his newly bleached hair attracting the now familiar "Match of the Dye" headlines, Beckham and the provisional squad flew to La Manga in Spain for training. It was here that manager Glenn Hoddle held his bizarre pre-tournament meetings in which he told individual players whether or not they were in the squad and which culminated in Gazza smashing up his room (although that only came out later when Hoddle published his controversial World Cup diary). When Beckham was called in he told him: "Obviously you're in and it's going to be a great tournament for you. You just have to concentrate."

Beckham thought no more of it. The whole squad had been upset and angered by the Gazza incident but Beckham had played in every qualifier, he had no reason to believe his place in the team was under threat. He'd even been to see faith healer Eileen Drewery and, when she placed her hands on his head, hadn't made Ray Parlour's mistake of asking for a "short back and sides, please".

But Hoddle was already making noises about Beckham's "focus". The England manager told the press he was worried about Beckham's temperament, stating with no lack of insight: "In David's case it's about how he reacts when the ball is dead. I don't want to see cards being bandied about for something that could have been controlled." Martin Samuel in the *Daily Express* concurred: "He must be careful to mind his temper on the world stage."

Fair enough, but Beckham believed the matter should not have been dealt with in the media. His club manager, Alex Ferguson, would never publicly criticise a player and he was confused, especially when it emerged that Hoddle was considering dropping him for England's first match against Tunisia and replacing him with Tottenham's injury-prone Darren Anderton.

"If I'm not in the team I will be totally gutted,' he told one journalist off the record, "It will, without doubt, be the most disappointing moment of my entire career." But Beckham's fears were justified when Hoddle announced the Tunisia team in front of the whole squad and he wasn't in it.

"There had been no warning or explanation," explains Beckham in *My World*. "Instead he asked me to go straight in and do a big press conference. I'm not very good at hiding my feelings so it was a very hard day for me."

In front of the world's media Beckham was clearly

On the bench for the pre-World Cup friendly v Morocco, but Beckham was expecting to be back in the team when the tournament kicked off.

distraught. Alex Ferguson was furious his player had been so publicly humiliated and United's youth team coach Eric Harrison, in France on a scouting mission, rushed to the team's hotel to offer the club's support. Later in the day Beckham confronted Hoddle for an explanation and was told the manager felt he lacked focus. "He said I wasn't focused and my mind was elsewhere."

Just before the World Cup David had been photographed on holiday with Victoria in St Tropez wearing a sarong. The Posh and Becks story still had the papers in a frenzy – "Three Lions on a Skirt" was the gleeful front page *Sun* headline – and Hoddle wouldn't be the first person to have questioned whether his relationship and his profile were impinging on his football. Beckham admits he missed his fiancée desperately when they were apart. He would spend hours on the phone to her, even from his mobile on the team coach, but he was flabbergasted at Hoddle's suggestion.

"In my mind it was ridiculous," he said later. "It was the World Cup. I'd been thinking about it since I was a kid. Although the players were unhappy about Gazza being left out and there was the talk about Eileen Drewery in the press, coming into the World Cup I was focused. I was ready to play. It was the World Cup. There is no player in the world who wouldn't be focused. Unfortunately the manager saw it differently."

Beckham's relationship with Hoddle was deteriorating to the point of no return. "It is important to feel that you can trust the manager but I was moping around the hotel not knowing what was happening or where I stood. I was devastated not to be playing."

England won the Tunisia game 2–0, and Hoddle stuck by the same team for the group's key match against Romania in Toulouse. However, with 30 minutes gone and England 1–0 down, Paul Ince had to go off with a badly gashed leg and Beckham was called into the fray, receiving a huge ovation from the massed ranks of England fans in the crowd which he later described as "absolutely staggering". England equalised with seven minutes to go thanks to sub Michael Owen, but Romania scored again in injury time. It was all down to the last match.

Despite the defeat Beckham had played well in midfield and kept his place for the crunch clash with Colombia. Playing in his favoured central role with Anderton outside him at right wing-back, Beckham was brilliant – he had finally arrived at the World Cup he had so badly wanted to grace. In the 33rd minute England, already 1–0 up, were awarded a free-kick outside the box. "A couple of players asked if I was going to have a crack," said Beckham the next day, "and I said 'just watch this'."

The England number 7 whipped the ball over the wall and into the net in a manner that had the brilliant Brazilian Roberto Carlos crowing about it in the papers the next day. "I don't know how he got that bend and power on this new ball," he exclaimed. England were into the next round and Beckham was undroppable. The whole of England was hailing the performances of Beckham and Owen, Hoddle telling the papers he had got the best out of Beckham by dropping him and insisting he'd always planned to play him in the Colombia match.

Glenn Hoddle had been a truly great player. Could it be that he was jealous of the attention Beckham was receiving, after all he had been largely overlooked by England during his career? At training the morning after the match with Colombia he asked Beckham to take a free-kick. Having had just a few hours sleep and not yet done any stretching, instead of hitting it with power Beckham just lobbed the ball softly over the wall. "Obviously you haven't got the ability to do that," said Hoddle in front of the whole team. He later apologised.

Whatever was going on between him and the manager, Beckham was bursting with anticipation for the biggest game of his life so far. He was all over the papers the day before the game. *The Sun* had him singing their version of "Don't Cry for me Argentina" on its front page and a quote from his future Man United team-mate, the Argentinian star Seba Veron, on the back, insisting: "Beckham is too handsome. In fact, he is so good-looking I don't know whether to kick him or kiss him."

It was a welcome comical aside in a build-up which had taken on an intensity beyond sport. The military overtones in the tabloid's weren't even insinuated, this was war alright with The Falklands

a glorious past victory and Maradona's "Hand of God" goal in 1986 a defeat to be avenged. Lord help anyone who makes a mistake in this match.

The rest, of course, is history. Argentina took the lead with a penalty, Shearer equalised from the spot then Beckham played in Owen to score the goal of the tournament before Zanetti made it 2–2 just before half-time. The second half had barely kicked off when Argentinian midfielder Diego Simeone clattered into the back of Beckham, knocking him to the ground.

"All I remember is that the ball was played up to me and I felt a shove in the back," remembers Beckham in *My World*. "Then I think the ball hit me in the face or chest and I felt a slap on the head or as if someone was pulling my hair and Simeone said something. If I had not lifted my right leg nothing would have happened and, to this day, I'm convinced I hardly touched him. But I just flicked my foot up instinctively, he went down and that was the start of it."

Time stood still. Did he really do that? Did the ref see it? Look at Beckham's face in the photos now and you can see the disbelief even in his own eyes. "It is hard talking about it even now," he says in *My World*. "Gary Neville came up to me as soon as it happened and said, 'what did you do that for?' I think he knew by the expression on the referee's face what was coming but I didn't expect the red card at all. I honestly thought I had hardly done anything but once he booked Simeone, I realised what was coming. Out came the red card."

Just as it had when he scored from the halfway line, Beckham's life took another dramatic course. Sitting with the England physio in the changing room he watched on TV as his ten team-mates hung on – and if Sol Campbell's goal hadn't been disallowed he might have been spared his public execution. He phoned Victoria who was watching in a New York bar, actually being filmed by a documentary crew when she took the call. "What's going on?" she pleaded. He watched from the tunnel as England went out of another tournament on penalties, and as the team trooped into the dressing room the only person to speak to him was Tony Adams. "Don't ever think you've let us down,"

insisted the Arsenal skipper. "You're a great player and I love you to bits."

"I went through every emotion," continues Beckham in *My World*. "I did get angry in the changing room, with myself and with the whole situation for a while but when we went to leave I felt numb. It was only when I saw my mum and dad as we were leaving the ground that I cracked up. That was rock bottom because I am quite an emotional person. I cried watching the film *Armageddon* and I get a lump in my throat just watching some reunion on a show like *Surprise Surprise*. But I had not cried like I did then since I was a child. For a good 10 minutes, I just lost it."

Meanwhile, at the after match press conference Hoddle was using Beckham as his "Get out of Jail Free" card. "That cost us dearly. I'm not denying that cost us the game," he said. Diego Simeone's comments were lost somewhere in the frenzy. "In reality he didn't do anything. I think he could have had a yellow card and that would have been enough." Adidas spent the night hastily tearing down billboard posters.

Beckham and the England team returned to their hotel, arriving back as the printing presses back home were starting to roll into action. "10 Heroic Lions – One Stupid Boy" screamed the *Daily Mirror* who also included a cut-out dartboard with Beckham's head as the bullseye. *The Star* subs chipped in with "Sorry boys no tits on page three today, just Beckham" and *The Telegraph* pompously pontificated: "Beckham's silly little, smart little kick at his Argentinian opponent was what's wrong with the national character." The papers were unanimous in their vitriol, and a wounded England had its scapegoat.

On the return flight to England Hoddle pulled Beckham aside and told him it was just one of those things, but the damage had been done. The words Alex Ferguson left on his answerphone undoubtedly carried more weight with Beckham. "It's in the past. Get back to Manchester where people love you and get playing football again," he said. But the wounds were too fresh, and when the England team landed back at Heathrow, Beckham booked himself straight onto a flight to New York to meet up with Victoria and escape the furore.

Right: Becks' first ever goal for England: the free-kick stunner against Colombia.
Pages 50/51: Beckham walks off after receiving the red card in Saint-Etienne.

Back home in the cold light of day, Hoddle began to backtrack. "There is hurt for him as an individual and us as a team. I would plead with people to think about the positive things he's done in an England shirt. It would be wrong for too many people in football to put blame on his shoulders."

It was too late. *The Sun* printed a picture of a Beckham effigy, complete with England shirt and sarong, that had been hung from a noose outside a south London pub. Of the 5,000 callers to a *Talk Radio* phone-in, 61 per cent said Beckham should never play for England again. Rent-a-quote pundit Alan Mullery insisted: "Beckham will never get over this." Random D Beckhams all over the country received abusive phone calls, as did David's parents Ted and Sandra who, in their son's absence, faced up to the full spite of the nation.

"I'm no longer proud to be British after what they've done to my son," said Ted Beckham, "all through a game of football. I'm just glad David's out of the country. He hasn't seen half of what's gone on and I won't let him."

Tony Blair intervened: "I should think that no one feels worse about it than David Beckham does, and he is obviously going to have to learn from that," he told Parliament, and even higher forces than the PM were spinning in on this one. "Remember, David Beckham is a human being just like me and you," urged Dr David Spriggs of the Bible Society.

"I know I've not always been an angel," said Beckham later, "there are some things I've done that I have regretted. But there were times after the World Cup when I was treated like a criminal."

Referee Kim Milton Nielsen was shocked, too, telling a Danish paper: "It's sick how people have reacted to what he did in the World Cup. You would think he had committed a terrible crime but it's only football not World War Three."

Even when Beckham publicly apologised in *The Sun* newspaper, the tabloids who missed out on the exclusive laid into him for making money out of it. They, of course, would have turned down the story.

"This is, without doubt, the worst moment of my career," he said, "and I will always regret what I did. I want every England supporter to know how sorry I am."

It was only in New York, where Victoria told him she was pregnant with the soon-to-be aptly named Brooklyn, that Beckham could escape the furore, although several papers tracked him down and photographed them shopping on Fifth Avenue.

So what of the future? Could Beckham ever return home? Barcelona were said to have tabled a £17 million bid and Real Madrid were also interested. Even Ted Beckham fuelled the speculation by questioning whether his son could ever play in England again.

Alex Ferguson had other ideas. He launched a vicious attack on Glenn Hoddle and the English media, using the situation to reinforce to Beckham that Mancheter United was his home and that's where he would be safe. United had always thrived on a siege mentality, and in some ways the anti-Beckham lobby was playing right into Ferguson's hands in his preparations for the season ahead.

In United's own magazine, respected football writer Oliver Holt speculated immaculately on Beckham's future, and his words resonate poignantly several years and a World Cup later. "Let us hope," wrote Holt back in August 1998, "that fate has not finished with Beckham yet. In the dizzying cycle of despair and delight that it has foisted upon him, he is due a spell of pure joy. The even-handed among the critics have voiced the hope that he will be able to take something positive from his dismissal and English football will be the richer if he can grow into the pre-eminent force his talents deserve.

"He will be mercilessly baited at other grounds and by the away fans who travel to Old Trafford when the season begins. United's first away match against West Ham United at Upton Park will probably be as severe a test as he will get.

"If he can survive, as survive he must, then David Beckham will emerge a better player on the other side. If he has learned that even one rash moment can mean ruin and despair, then he will be an even more potent force as a footballer than he was before.

"Undoubtedly there are those who will be hoping that the sending off in Saint-Etienne will set a sorry trend for David Beckham. Those who care about the future of English football, though, are praying it will be the making of the man."

Beckham moves in mysterious ways.

MANSFIELD ROAD BAPTIST CHURCH

- GOD FORGIVES
EVEN
DAVID BECKHAM •

the
season
when it
all went
right

Several hours after Manchester United had won the Champions League final, and completed the Treble on a night of extraordinary drama at the Nou Camp, David Beckham finally steps out of the United dressing room holding the European Cup. He has taken it upon himself to chaperone the grand old silver trophy to the team's banquet at the Arts Hotel on the Barcelona seafront.

Dressed in the grey Versace club suit he had chosen for the whole team, and with his winners' medal around his neck (he later admitted he didn't take it off for several days), Beckham walks down the crowded tunnel, stopping to talk to the world's media, but never letting the trophy out of his sight.

When he reaches the car park at the end of the tunnel, he surveys a surprisingly quiet scene. It is at this moment that he turns around and sees his father. The pair had not arranged to meet here, but no words are exchanged before Beckham places the European Cup at his feet and embraces his father.

"Dad didn't need to say a word and we just hugged," Beckham recalled later. "It felt like he was crying or, at least, trying hard not to. And my eyes were pricking too. The two of us knew what it had been like when we'd met less than a year before, in another car park, after the Argentina game at the World Cup in Saint-Etienne. My parents knew better than anybody what had happened to me since that night."

What had happened was that Beckham had played a leading role in Manchester United sweeping all before them to win the Premiership, the FA Cup and the Champions League that season. But more importantly, over the past year, Beckham had also transformed the public's perception of him. He was no longer a "stupid boy" as one newspaper had branded him after he had been sent off at the World

Cup; he was now a hero, a winner, and a member of what had become England's greatest-ever club side.

"That season was the most incredible season any of us, maybe any footballer playing in England, will ever experience," says Beckham. "I will spend the rest of my career trying to equal it because that night in the Nou Camp was the greatest feeling I have known on a football pitch."

Only eight months earlier, Beckham admitted he had started the season, "not sure about whether I'd make it through to the following May in one piece."

He was still being vilified for his World Cup red card, and throughout the summer of 1998 he had been portrayed as the player who had let the whole nation down, a spoilt pretty boy who couldn't be trusted on the big occasion. A sarong-wearing effigy of Beckham was hung up outside a London pub, a David Beckham hatred society was founded on the internet and Arsenal fans greeted him at the 1998/99 curtain-raising Charity Shield at Wembley with a banner that read, "David Beckscum".

This deluge of abuse forced Beckham to think seriously about leaving English football, but on the eve of the new season he signed a new five-year contract, worth an estimated £7 million, that would keep him at Old Trafford until the summer of 2003. He was happy to stay for the moment, but as admitted later, "I went in to the season feeling that in the aftermath of the World Cup this was make or break for me, at least as far as playing my football in England was concerned."

Manchester United's first game of the 1998/99 season was against Leicester City at Old Trafford, and Beckham was worried about how the United fans would react to him. "I don't think I've ever been as nervous before a football match," he confesses. "I was dreading those 90 minutes."

26 May 1999, Camp Nou, Barcelona: Beckham and Dwight Yorke celebrate Manchester United's remarkable 2–1 European Cup final win over Bayern Munich.

His fears evaporated as soon as he jogged on to the pitch and was given a rapturous welcome. The message was simple one: You are back among those who love you.

Beckham has described this outpouring of affection as an "amazing feeling". United struggled though, and with only 11 minutes remaining they were losing 2–0. With time running out Beckham gave United some hope by whipping in a cross for Teddy Sheringham to pull a goal back, before United then won a free kick 30 yards from goal in the very last minute of the game.

"I stepped up and there was this hush around the ground: just silence," Beckham recalls. "The only voice I could hear was one in my head, 'Please go in, Please, please go in'."

Beckham's prayers were answered when his shot sailed over the wall and past the outstretched hand of the Leicester goalkeeper Peggy Arphexad. 2–2. He had salvaged a point and ran to the United fans with an expression of joy and relief all over his face.

But Beckham still had to travel away from home. And he really would have winced when he saw United's first away game of the season was a trip to Upton Park. West Ham fans have never had any trouble whipping themselves into a frenzy for Manchester United games and now they had a cause to rally around: the hounding of David Beckham.

The menacing build-up to this game had begun the moment Beckham trooped off the pitch with his head bowed against Argentina in Saint-Etienne. Sir Alex Ferguson tried to play it down, saying:

"Unless they are selling new lungs down there then there's nothing they can do other than shout. That's what they always do. It can't be any worse than it normally is. It is always fierce down there."

But despite the West Ham manager Harry Redknapp and club legend Sir Geoff Hurst both appealing for calm, West Ham fans still gave Beckham a special East End "welcome".

"I'll never forget arriving at Upton Park ... They were waiting for me out in the car park: hundreds of people, anger all over their faces," recalls Beckham.

Out on the pitch, Beckham's every touch of the ball was booed and he vivdly remembers the looks of hatred on the contorted faces of the West Ham fans:

It said to Beckham, "If we could, we'd have you."

But Beckham came through the game, a rather dull goalless draw, unscathed and so passed what would be one of his greatest challenges of the season. He also earned the further respect of his boss.

"David has held up well following his ordeal," said Sir Alex Ferguson. "It can't be easy when you are vilified by a nation, but once back in the fold at Old Trafford where he's safe, he revealed the strength of character I believe is the hallmark of a Manchester United player."

This character was being revealed more and more in the autumn of 1998 as Beckham and his team-mates began to show the first signs of potential greatness. Despite being placed in the same Champions League group as fellow European superpowers Barcelona and Bayern Munich, United progressed to the quarter-finals stage without losing a single game. United drew both home and away against Barcelona and Bayern, while slaughtering the Danish champions Brondby 5–0 and 6–2.

Beckham looked utterly at ease on the European stage, and scored stunning free-kicks against both Barcelona and Brondby at Old Trafford.

"He has such brilliant ability that there was no way I could get to the ball," confessed Barcelona's beaten goalkeeper Ruud Hesp. "I doubt there is a keeper in the would who could stop him."

Despite Beckham's growing reputation, he was still troubled. He struggled to cope with the merciless booing whenever he stepped on to a pitch (even by his own fans when he returned for England). In November 1998, he gave his first major interview since the World Cup to Manchester United's official magazine, and came across as cowered and battered by the whole experience.

At the turn of the year, Alex Ferguson wisely decided to give Beckham a three-week rest. It had the desired effect. In his first two games after his return to the first team, Beckham helped United to beat Leicester City 6–2 at Filbert Street and to engineer a dramatic 2–1 victory over Liverpool in the fourth round of the FA Cup after United had been losing with just two minutes remaining. This would later prove to be a very useful trick.

It seemed almost inevitable that David Beckham

Less than a year after being sent off in the World Cup and being dismissed as a "stupid boy", Beckham was floating on air, a Treble winner.

would come face-to-face with his Argentinian nemesis Diego Simeone, so there was little surprise when United were drawn to play Simeone's Inter Milan in the quarter-finals of the Champions League.

Unrelenting hype swirled around the pair's reunion, but Beckham ignored it all to deliver one of his best-ever performances for United. He set up both goals for Dwight Yorke in a 2–0 first leg win with a couple of wonderful crosses as part of an overall display that had his manager purring.

"Beckham was outstanding," declared Ferguson. "David is the best crosser of the ball in Europe and he was back to his best."

The evening's pantomime villain, Diego Simeone was reduced to a mere sideshow ("I thought the crowd would boo me a lot more, but there was little noise for me," said the forlorn Argentinian). The nearest he got to Beckham all night was at the final whistle when they embraced and swapped shirts. And just like the previous 90 minutes, Beckham handled this with composure and maturity.

"I decided it was a nice way to end it all after so much had been said about the two of us," he said. "It's in the past now."

The following morning, Beckham had little time to read the newspapers' triumphant headlines ("Beckham's glory night", "A night of sweet revenge" and "Beckham's art is his salvation,") as his fiancée Victoria, who he would marry in a lavish ceremony that summer, went in to labour and gave birth to a baby boy who they named Brooklyn.

Fatherhood only seemed to add to Beckham's increasing on-pitch maturity. Two weeks later, in the return leg against Inter Milan at the San Siro, Beckham again refused to be provoked by the Italians as United secured a 1–1 draw to progress in to the Champions League semi-finals, and in an FA Cup quarter-final replay against Chelsea at Stamford Bridge, Beckham responded to the home fans' taunts by blowing them a kiss.

Next up was Arsenal in the FA Cup semi-final. The first game at Villa Park had ended in a goalless draw, forcing the teams to return to Birmingham four days later for the replay:

"I remember sitting in the dressing room 40 minutes ahead of kick-off and thinking, 'I've never

scored against them. What would it feel like to get a goal against Arsenal?'."

He didn't have to wait too long to find out as he curled a wonderful strike past David Seaman to give United the lead after only 15 minutes. Arsenal would equalise through Dennis Bergkamp before Ryan Giggs conjured up his famous solo goal in extra-time to put United through to the FA Cup final. Beckham finished the evening being hoisted up on to the shoulders of a posse of celebrating United fans and carried around the pitch.

Although they dared not talk about it, Beckham and his team-mates were all becoming aware that a momentum was building towards the Treble.

"Every game we played during the last couple of months was a cup final: if we had lost any game, in the League, the FA Cup or in Europe, it would have meant the Treble had gone," recalls Beckham. "We were on the kind of roll where you would finish one game and the adrenaline kidded you into believing you could play another one the following day."

It was this adrenaline that saw United overcome Juventus after two enthralling Champions League semi-final legs to make it to their first final for 31 years. In the first leg at Old Trafford, Beckham provided the lofted pass for Giggs to score United's late equaliser in a 1–1 draw. United coach Steve McClaren revealed that Beckham covered 14km that night:

"Of the 22 players on the park, David ran the most by a long way. He also delivered the most passes. His contribution was enormous."

In the second leg at the Stadio delle Alpi, United went 2–0 down to the Italians after only 11 minutes.

"But it didn't feel like we were out of it," Beckham said later. "I remember turning to Gary Neville and saying, 'They're not that good, Gaz. We can win this.'."

Beckham helped to start United's comeback with the cross for United's first goal, a Roy Keane header, and they would go on to score twice more to grasp a 3–2 win on the night. The only disappointment for United were bookings for Keane and Paul Scholes which meant they would be suspended for the final.

Back in the Premiership, on the last day of the season United needed to beat Tottenham Hotspur at Old Trafford to be sure of reclaiming the title. It was the London side who scored first through Les

Beckham and best mate Gary Neville wave
to friends and family in the crowd.

Ferdinand, forcing United to frantically search for an equaliser. It arrived just before half-time when Beckham scored an exquisite goal from a tight angle.

"I watched the video of the game later and the look on my face after I scored that goal gave me a bit of a shock," Beckham says. "I don't think I've ever seen it before: that desire, wanting to win so badly; it looked like fury. It was all the frustration of the first half coming out, along with the tension of knowing what was at stake. I just ran off towards the supporters screaming."

Beckham would have even more cause to scream when substitute Andy Cole scored United's winner in the second half to confirm United as champions and complete the first leg of the Treble.

The second leg was a strangely simple affair with Newcastle offering little resistance in the FA Cup final at Wembley. United strolled to a 2–0 win with goals from Teddy Sheringham and Paul Scholes.

With just four days until the Champions League final, Sir Alex Ferguson had considered resting Beckham at Wembley, but he played him and was rewarded with a superb performance.

"People think that going to Barcelona without Keane will be a major problem, but I don't think so after seeing how magnificently Beckham played," opined the United manager.

Beckham says he felt relaxed before what was by far the biggest game of his career, the Champions League final against Bayern Munich in Barcelona, but admits the game "was all a bit of a nightmare". The Germans took the lead after only six minutes and held on to it. Beckham played in central midfield in place of the suspended Keane, and while he believes he played "pretty well", the rest of his United team-mates certainly didn't. In fact, Bayern Munich should have extended their lead.

"All these chances, why haven't they scored again?" Beckham remembers thinking. "Keep going and you never know. This could still happen for us."

But it hadn't by the time the fourth official held up his board to indicate normal time was over and there would only be three minutes of stoppage time.

"I was convinced that was it," he remembers. "I just felt gutted. It was one of the worst moments I had experienced on a football pitch. I even saw the trophy up in the stands with Bayern Munich

ribbons already on it."

Soon after United won a corner in front of their own fans crammed into the three tiers of the Nou Camp. Beckham rushed over to take it, telling himself: "Don't mess this up. Just float it in and try to put it in a dangerous area." He did just that, and the ball bounced around in the area like a pinball until Teddy Sheringham guided it in from close range. Beckham, his team-mates and all the United substitutes piled into a joyous heap behind the goal.

"I just went mad and I swear I felt like crying," says Beckham. "At that moment, it felt like the whole season caught up with us. I was shattered."

As thoughts immediately turned to extra-time, United won another corner on the same side of the pitch. Beckham managed to summon up enough strength to whip the ball in to the area, where Teddy Sheringham glanced it on and there was Ole Gunnar Solskjaer, sticking out his leg to win the game in the very last minute. The final whistle blew moments later to confirm United as European champions and winners of the Treble.

"The sound of that whistle was like an electric shock and I got this last burst of energy," Beckham says. "I sprinted with my arms stretched out beside me almost the length of the pitch and down to our fans... I don't know if I will experience moments, or see celebrations, quite like those ever again."

These celebrations went on all night, starting with the presentation of the European Cup, which was followed by an hour-long private party between United's players and fans on the pitch, before the team retreated into the dressing room and then moved on with their families and friends to a banquet. There were no more games now, and Beckham could finally reflect on the greatest season of his career. The year-long journey that started with the shame of Saint-Etienne hanging over him had ended with him as a Treble winner tearfully hugging his father in the car park at the Nou Camp.

"This has been the best ever year of my life, one I will never forget," Beckham would say at the beginning of the following season. "I have loved every minute of it: having Brooklyn, getting married to Victoria and winning three trophies with United. I couldn't have designed a better year. Without a doubt I am happier than I've ever been."

"Look at me, Dad, I'm on top of the world!"

the
most
unlikely
england
captain
ever?

While the 1998/99 season was one of storming success for David Beckham at club level, his post-World Cup international performances were unspectacular by comparison. There was a sense that he was going through a rehabilitation process, attempting to build bridges with the England fans who were so dismayed by his red card in Saint-Etienne.

However, Glenn Hoddle, the England head coach, whose main aim should have been to calm the furore, did little to stem the flow of anti-Beckham vitriol. Hoddle's World Cup diary, published shortly after the tournament, hit the headlines by publicly hanging out England favourite Paul Gascoigne to dry. What attracted slightly less publicity was the manager's attitude towards the Manchester United number 7's dismissal against Argentina.

On the one hand Hoddle appeared keen to protect Beckham. "I was determined to stress that David shouldn't be made a scapegoat for what happened," he wrote. But, in self-contradictory mode, he added: "If he hadn't got sent off we would have had 11 men on the pitch and would have won the game."

It was clear who Hoddle really blamed for England's World Cup exit. Convinced of his own omniscience, he believed he could see the way ahead for Beckham.

"Counselling of some sort would help, perhaps from Eileen Drewery," the England manager advised without the slightest hint of irony.

Despite Hoddle's reservations about Beckham's temperament and possibly even his ability, David was recalled to the England set-up as soon as he had served his ban for the red card. And he performed adequately in an uninspiring 3–0 victory over lowly Luxembourg on 14 October as England's push to qualify for Euro 2000 began to gather momentum.

A month later Beckham appeared in a friendly win over the Czech Republic. It was his last game under Hoddle, who left the England manager's job early in 1999 "by mutual consent" following derogatory remarks he had made about disabled people. Hoddle's supercilious demeanour and poor results on the field meant his departure was inevitable; his ill-judged comments merely afforded the Football Association the pretext to show him the door.

Understandably, the FA was keen to recruit a manager with renowned communication skills as his successor. They persuaded Kevin Keegan, then in charge of ambitious Fulham, to take the job on a temporary basis. It was to nobody's surprise that the former Newcastle boss was eventually unable to resist the offer of a permanent post.

The England camp was a far happier place under Keegan, whose enthusiasm and relative humility made him popular with the players. Results also improved and England swept through to the European Championship finals after beating Scotland 2–1 on aggregate in the play-offs.

Euro 2000, staged in the Low Countries, was an important landmark in the development of the national team and its most famous player. Beckham received widespread public sympathy for the appalling abuse he received from a pocket of mindless England fans at their tournament opener against Portugal in Eindhoven.

England raced to an early 2–0 lead with Paul Scholes and Steve McManaman converting crosses dextrously delivered by Beckham's right boot. But Luis Figo and Rui Costa inspired a memorable comeback as the Portuguese claimed a 3–2 victory.

Beckham was England's brightest spark on a disappointing night, but as he made his way towards the tunnel at the final whistle, a group of England fans who had barracked the players throughout,

Beckham trudges off the pitch after his first game for England following his World Cup trauma, a 3–0 win over minnows Luxembourg in October 1998.

subjected him to a shocking volley of insults about his wife Victoria and young son, Brooklyn. In most circumstances, Beckham's reaction, a one-fingered salute (see chapter opener), would have brought condemnation from the authorities. But as Kevin Keegan argued, no one can be expected to contain their emotions in the face of such a vile and unwarranted onslaught and the vast majority of England fans agreed.

A turning point had been reached in Beckham's relationship with England supporters.

"I know that there will always be some people who will abuse me, but I think what happened at Euro 2000 when my wife and son got the worst stick imaginable has made a few people stop and think," said Beckham later.

Individually, Beckham performed well in a disappointing tournament for the England team (defeat by Romania meant they failed to qualify for the knockout stage) and he was instrumental in England's first defeat of Germany in international competition since 1966.

"Beckham has great vision and we must put a man on him all the time to stop him getting in those dangerous crosses," Franz Beckenbauer warned his compatriots before the match in Charleroi, Belgium. But it was advice that was not heeded until Bayern Munich met Manchester United in the European Cup the following season.

Beckham had entered Euro 2000 in great shape. ("I went into Euro 2000 in better form than France '98," he admitted to Manchester United's official magazine afterwards). The midfielder had enjoyed another profitable season with Manchester United as the club clinched a second Premiership title in as many years. Still, the 1999/2000 campaign wasn't without controversy. Once again, Beckham received negative publicity for a red card, this time against Mexican side Necaxa in FIFA's inaugural World Club Championship, hosted by Brazil in January 2000. The dismissal itself was harsh – Beckham's lunge at Jose Milian was clumsy, not malicious – and appeared to have more to do with the player's apparent reputation than the challenge itself.

Media reaction to the incident was predictably exaggerated and Beckham fans who were unable to make the trip to Brazil were left particularly exasperated by the sanctimonious rants of BBC commentator Barry Davies. United slipped out of the tournament after defeat to local side Vasco da Gama, Beckham's destiny as England captain seemed further away than ever.

Back on English turf, United prospered. Ferguson's men clearly felt the benefit of what was ultimately a restful trip to Brazil. They had expected to play catch-up in the league, but their main rivals, especially Arsenal, had faltered in the champions' absence. United lost only once more in the Premiership as they charged to title glory. Beckham performed admirably throughout despite missing the game at Leeds on 20 February (see chapter nine) and was on the scoresheet with a trademark curling free-kick as United wrapped up the title with victory at Southampton on 22 April.

Still, a feeling of anti-climax lingered around Old Trafford. United's stated intention was to dominate European football by winning the Champions League repeatedly, but they failed to retain their crown. The team's tendency to over-commit in attack, especially at home, exposing a shaky defence was ruthlessly exploited by Real Madrid.

The Champions League quarter-final first leg at the Santiago Bernabeu on 4 April ended goalless. Beckham and co were expected to storm to victory back on home ground 15 days later. But Ferguson was outwitted by Madrid manager Vicente del Bosque, who cunningly eschewed his usual 4–4–2 formation in favour of a 3–5–2 system that allowed wing-backs Michel Salgado and Roberto Carlos to cause United plenty of problems on the flanks.

Not for the last time, the Brazilian gave Beckham an arduous evening and the visitors raced to a 3–0 advantage after an unfortunate own goal by Roy Keane and a typically stylish brace from Raul.

United struck back with commendable spirit. Beckham scored one of the finest and most uncharacteristic goals of his career, jinking through several tackles before slamming an unstoppable shot past Iker Casillas. Paul Scholes then converted a late penalty but United ran out of time and exited the competition to the eventual winners.

Post-Madrid, Ferguson clearly recognised his

Buoyed by his Treble success with Manchester United, Beckham steams into action for England v Sweden in a Euro 2000 qualifier, 5 June 1999.

68

team's limitations and immediately sought to rectify them. A world-class goalscorer was required and United agreed a £19 million fee with PSV Eindhoven for their brilliant young striker Ruud van Nistelrooy. Unfortunately, the deal was put on hold for 12 months until the Dutchman had recovered from a serious knee injury. In French international goalkeeper Fabien Barthez, a £7.8 million signing from Monaco, Ferguson also felt he'd found the true successor to Peter Schmeichel.

But the 2000/2001 season would again see United and Beckham cruise to triumph in the domestic game yet fail in European competition. The Premiership trophy stayed in Manchester for a third consecutive year as Arsenal proved unable to match United's consistency. Beckham certainly pulled his weight, contributing numerous assists for the likes of Andrew Cole, Teddy Sheringham, Dwight Yorke and Paul Scholes to score, as well as six goals of his own.

Yet Beckham's performances on the European stage mirrored the team's struggles at this level – he even failed to score for the only time in nine seasons of European football at Old Trafford. United had a comfortable passage through the second group phase, only to fall at the quarter-final stage again, this time to a Bayern Munich team eager to avenge their painful Barcelona '99 defeat.

The German side won the tie convincingly, their tactic to shackle wide midfielders, Beckham and Ryan Giggs, effectively cutting off the supply line to United's strikers. In the home leg, Beckham was especially well marshalled by French international full-back Bixente Lizarazu and both men received cautions, meaning they missed the return match. In the Frenchman's case that represented a job well done and United crashed out of the competition after a 2–1 defeat in Munich.

Even if his main shortcoming – the inability to beat his opposite number – had been exposed by Bayern Munich, the 2000/2001 season ended on a high note for Beckham with a comprehensive 2–0 victory over Greece in Athens on 6 June. It was a third successive World Cup qualifying win under Sven-Göran Eriksson, who had become the fourth man to manage England in just over two years .

The previous October, England's qualifying campaign for Japan/Korea 2002 had suffered a disastrous setback when they lost their opening game to old rivals Germany. Beckham was the only person who performed well in a dismal England display that did nothing to celebrate the occasion of the last-ever international at Wembley and which led to Kevin Keegan's immediate resignation.

On the positive side, the crowd was heard to chant: "Come on, Beckham. Come on, Beckham" rather than the traditional "Come on, England. Come on, England."

It was clear evidence that fans were beginning to realise Beckham's importance to the team, his commitment to the cause and the fact that he was not the troublesome brat the media had portrayed him as during the fallout to France '98.

Incredibly, his next match for England was as captain. Peter Taylor was rewarded for his outstanding work with the Under-21s by being handed the job of picking and preparing the full England team for a friendly against Italy in Turin on 15 November. The FA had already lined up Sven-Göran Eriksson, the Swedish manager of Italian giants Lazio, as Keegan's long-term successor, but Taylor was to fill the void in the meantime.

Taylor boldly selected a team of young players, and even more boldly selected David Beckham as his captain. Taylor's decision surprised a lot of observers but won instant support, especially when Beckham calmly diffused an unsavoury incident in which Gennaro Gattuso, the Italy midfielder, swung a fist in his direction.

"I saw David walk away, which was first-class on his part," said Taylor in praise of his captain.

However, on two fronts, David Beckham was the most unlikely man ever to wear the armband for England. On the one hand, he had had to win over the armies of England supporters who were reluctant to forgive him for his World Cup red card, something he achieved in the best way possible – by playing outstanding football. Beckham himself later admitted that he had reckoned the Argentina sending-off would preclude him from ever wearing the armband:

"If someone had told me after the 1998 World Cup that I would be leading my country out within three

Right: Happy days are here again; Pages 72/73: Beckham celebrates Paul Scholes' opening goal in the 2–0 World Cup qualifying win over Greece, 6 June 2001.

years, I would have laughed in their face."

Then there was the fact that few people regarded him as a natural-born leader. England captains like Beckham's own hero Bryan Robson and Tony Adams had one thing in common: they were tub-thumpers, men who led from the front, who showed controlled aggression in the face of intimidation. How could a shy, sarong-wearing man with a reputation for petulance have the authority to lead England. Beckham wasn't even regarded as a realistic candidate for club captaincy.

But from the outset it was clear that the honour of captaining his country provided extra motivation for the midfielder. His crucial winning goal against Finland at Anfield in his first competitive match as skipper, a World Cup qualifier, was just his second at international level, in his 39th appearance. Remarkably, Beckham's goalscoring record in his next 20 internationals was a goal every other game.

Beckham had openly pleaded for Liverpool fans attending the game to forget their club's traditional enmity with Manchester United and support him as England captain. The Kop responded magnificently.

Victoria Beckham was not at Anfield to witness the sea change in the England supporters' attitude towards her husband. David had insisted Victoria and Brooklyn stay away because he was concerned they might be abused by Liverpool fans. As it was, the new England skipper left the field to the strains of: "There's only one David Beckham."

The media response to Beckham's heroics was equally overwhelming.

"Thank God it's over: the scapegoating and hounding of a decent footballer and father who shows signs of finally blossoming as an international performer," wrote Paul Hayward in the *Daily Telegraph*. Meanwhile, the *Daily Mirror*, which had run the headline "Ten heroic lions and one stupid boy" after Beckham's World Cup dismissal, declared: "Fatherhood made a man of Beckham."

After England had triumphed 3–1 in Albania four days later, Beckham declared a new-found confidence in his ability to lead England: "There's a new authority in my game. I am a natural leader."

Beckham's 2000/2001 season finished with a trip to Athens, where England had to beat Greece to keep alive their hopes of competing in the following year's World Cup. In the weeks prior to the 6 June fixture, Sven-Göran Eriksson discovered the true lunacy that exists within British tabloid newspapers. Beckham was sporting a new Mohawk hairstyle and several papers ran articles suggesting that, as England captain, this was hardly the example to be setting to youngsters.

One tabloid enlisted rent-a-quote Brian Clough to give his view. "What Beckham has done is an abuse of privilege and office," the former Nottingham Forest manager ranted.

Eriksson, ever the broad-minded pragmatist, gave the matter short shrift: "As long as he is a good captain and a good player I'm very happy. It's up to him how he cuts his hair."

The England skipper delivered the perfect riposte to his detractors with an excellent performance and another priceless goal as England overcame Greece.

"It's great I'm finally scoring regularly for England," Beckham said after scoring with a delightful swerving free-kick. "I feel more liberated as captain and I'm playing with much more freedom."

In his opening games as England manager, Sven-Göran Eriksson was clearly vindicated in his decision to retain Beckham as captain.

"I'm very happy with the way David has responded," the Swede enthused after the Greece victory. "He is behaving like a true captain. He is scoring great goals and playing good football."

A strong bond was developing between coach and captain, with Beckham reflecting Eriksson's cool, considered approach to the game. Ironically, Beckham had originally been opposed to the appointment of a foreign coach. But the midfielder soon realised that he was benefiting from the Swede's influence.

"The job of captain is very easy under Sven because of the coolness and calmness that he has brought the team," Beckham revealed in his book *My World*. "I think we have struck up a very good relationship and I enjoy talking to him about the game."

But while Beckham and Eriksson continued to strike an excellent rapport, the relationship between the player and his club manager was deteriorating.

Beckham completed the remarkable transformation from national hate figure to England's captain and talisman in less than three years.

In the late 1990s, the marketing men for a well-known brand of lager dreamt up a television advert that claimed the beverage had special properties. It was based on the vociferous pundit Jimmy Hill being left speechless by an England first-half performance that saw them take a healthy lead over old rivals Germany. On 1 September 2001, the dream became reality: England thrashed Germany in Munich.

The hosts took an early lead only for England to strike back with a Michael Owen hat-trick and goals from Steven Gerrard and Emile Heskey. England displayed a rare streak of ruthlessness in exploiting Germany's slow defensive line and the team deserved the plaudits of a nation that now believed a place in the 2002 World Cup finals was theirs.

Beckham's personal performance was one of culture and maturity despite sustaining a groin injury during Manchester United's draw at Aston Villa just six days earlier. That he was prepared to play through the pain barrier earned him extra popularity with England fans and the media.

"This was perhaps the seminal moment in making the boy David the man who leads his country," opined Ian McGarry in the *Daily Mail*.

However, the wave of triumphalism that spread through the country in the four days between the famous victory in Germany and England's next appointment, against Albania at St James's Park, Newcastle, did little to help Sven-Göran Eriksson keep his men fully focused.

Albania made life hard for England by sitting deep and indulging in ample gamesmanship, much of which was directed at Beckham. But the captain was unperturbed and England eventually found the goals, through Michael Owen and Robbie Fowler, to secure victory.

Sven-Göran Eriksson's team now sat on top of their group and knew that as long as they achieved the same result against Greece in the last round of matches as the Germans managed against Finland, they would be through to Japan/Korea 2002.

The scriptwriter for the finale to England's World Cup qualifying campaign clearly possessed a romantic streak. The venue for the Greece match was Beckham's beloved Old Trafford and not even in his wildest reverie could Beckham have envisaged the Roy of the Rovers-style heroics he produced to drag his country to success. As his team-mates faltered, performing as if the weight of the world rested upon their shoulders, their captain played with complete freedom.

Beckham racked up an incredible 16km during the match, hounding opponents, running into space, tackling, passing, shooting and generally making up for his colleagues' deficiencies. This was a moment of destiny, the opportunity to prove beyond doubt that his rehabilitation from France '98 was complete.

Greece also played with an air of liberation. The visitors' campaign was over and only pride was at stake. They took a first-half lead, which was eventually cancelled out by substitute Teddy Sheringham from, of course, an expertly-delivered Beckham free-kick. But the Greeks struck again almost immediately.

With 92 minutes on the clock, a free-kick was awarded to the home side. Sheringham tried to usher Beckham aside, after seeing the skipper miss with eight previous pots at goal. Beckham pulled rank.

"When I got my last chance, Teddy Sheringham said he would have it but I decided I'd take it," he revealed in the post-match press conference.

Beckham placed the ball 30 yards from goal, to keeper Nikopolidis's right. After retreating the usual

Beckham celebrates after he almost singlehandedly earned his country a crucial 2–2 draw v Greece in England's final 2002 World Cup qualifier, 6 October 2001.

79

number of steps, he glanced up at the goal before concentrating on the ball and, with arms extended in characteristic fashion, propelled the perfect swerving free-kick into the top corner of the net.

"I told the referee to blow the whistle," Beckham joked after securing his country's World Cup place.

In the warm afterglow of Beckham's finest hour, everyone who was anyone in football was being asked for their opinion of a national hero. Former Scotland international Kenny Dalglish declared that Beckham was capable of leading England to the ultimate World Cup triumph. "I would go so far as to say Beckham is already one of the great players," he added. Meanwhile, Pele, the greatest of them all, advised Eriksson to allow Beckham the central midfield berth he had long cherished.

"I would organise the team and let him run free," insisted the Brazilian legend.

The following spring, with the hype surrounding Beckham already at fever pitch, the question became not where or how he would play at the World Cup but whether he would participate at all.

In April 2002, Manchester United were drawn against Deportivo La Coruña in the quarter-finals of the Champions League. United produced their best display of the season to outwit Deportivo 2–0 in the first leg in Spain. Beckham had broken the deadlock with a spectacular, dipping 30-yard strike and had, for once, reproduced the world-class form he was managing regularly at international level.

But in the dying seconds of the match, Deportivo striker Diego Tristan slid in with a late and dangerous challenge on England skipper, who was stretchered from the field amid fears of a broken bone in his foot.

Happily, there was no break and Beckham recovered quickly to take his place in the United line-up for the return match eight days later. Again he looked sharp when a wild, two-footed challenge from Deportivo's Argentine midfielder Aldo Duscher caught the United player's left foot. This time there was a fracture, to Beckham's metatarsal, a tiny bone in the foot. The injury was to prove the focus of England's entire World Cup warm-up programme.

The immediate reaction of several of the country's less scrupulous tabloid newspapers was to hound Duscher around Spain. One even printed his telephone number and instructed readers to call and abuse him. But Beckham, with the diplomacy befitting an England captain, agreed to a stage-managed telephone apology from the Argentine hardman. Thus, the potential for long-lasting bad blood between the two players was extinguished.

Meanwhile, Prime Minister Tony Blair, never one to miss a publicity opportunity, expressed his concern about the health of the nation's footballing talisman.

"Nothing is more important to England's arrangements for the World Cup than the state of David Beckham's foot," Blair informed his Cabinet.

The editor of *The Sun* agreed as the newspaper published a picture of the injured foot on its front page and implored readers to: "Lay your hands on David's foot at noon and make it better." All very Eileen Drewery.

Beckham was determined to make a quick recovery. He followed the advice of the Manchester United medical staff, the England team doctors and an army of specialists to the letter. He slept in a hypoxic tent to maintain his fitness levels. This simulates the effect of being at high altitude where the body adapts to the lack of oxygen by increasing production of red blood cells, which, in short, speeds up the healing process.

With such a vast support network to help his rehabilitation, Becks was back behind the wheel of his Mercedes just a fortnight after breaking his foot. By this stage, the prognosis was good. Beckham's recovery was on course and medical experts expected him to be available for England's World Cup campaign, which was due to start on 2 June.

However, on the day Beckham was able to drive again, his World Cup hopes were nearly dashed by a freak accident. The midfielder was involved in a car crash. The nation held its breath, until Victoria appeared at the door of their home in Hertfordshire to allay fears of further damage to her husband's foot.

May was a happier month for the Beckhams. While Manchester United's season tailed off in the disappointment of losing the title to Arsenal and being eliminated from the semi-finals of the Champions League by Bayer Leverkusen, Beckham finally signed a new £15 million three-year contract.

Big in Japan: thousands of Japanese Beckham devotees became honorary England supporters during World Cup 2002 in tribute to their idol.

And by the second week of May, Beckham was running again. Meanwhile, his boot sponsors, Adidas, disclosed that they had spent £10,000 developing a reinforced boot to protect his fragile metartarsal from further damage.

The domestic season over, England's World Cup preparations began in earnest. Beckham accompanied his colleagues to a light-training camp/team-bonding session in Dubai. The day before the squad left for the Middle East, the Beckhams hosted a lavish farewell party, a charity event that was attended by 350 guests. The festivities apparently cost the Beckhams a cool £350,000.

According to newspaper reports, Sir Alex Ferguson tried to stop the England captain going on the Dubai trip in the belief that travelling such a long distance at a crucial stage in the recovery process could set back his rehabilitation. But Tord Grip, Eriksson's assistant, was quick to dispel rumours of a rift between the England coach and the Manchester United manager.

"We have been in touch with United every step of the way," Grip insisted. "David has already been working in the gym and swimming, but he needs to start running and ultimately kicking a ball."

That he did not do until 26 May, just a week before England's opening encounter of the World Cup. Eriksson's men played warm-up matches in South Korea against the Koreans themselves and Cameroon in Japan. Both matches were drawn and after the second, thousands of ecstatic Japanese fans stayed behind to applaud David as he was finally able to display his ball skills again.

Beckham was delighted to be nearing full fitness. In the days when there were serious doubts about his ability to participate in the World Cup he had revealed just how crucial his sporting career remains.

"The most important thing to me is my family, but without my football I'm a lost man," he admitted.

On 29 May, the nation finally received the good news it had been hoping for. David Beckham would be fit to face Sweden.

The national hysteria regarding Beckham's fitness was, in the eyes of many observers, reflected in Sven-Göran Eriksson's discernible lack of a contingency plan. For the Swede, Beckham's absence would be a major catastrophe. Such was Eriksson's reliance on Beckham that the England coach even considered taking his captain to the World Cup in a non-playing capacity.

"In life you have to gamble sometimes," said Eriksson. "For this kind of player you're more willing to take a risk."

Beckham and Eriksson had clearly developed the kind of close relationship, based on respect and understanding, that the player no longer enjoyed with his club manager, Sir Alex Ferguson.

"I don't know if you can find anyone better in the world today. He is very important to us," Eriksson purred in Japan.

Sadly, the clash with Sweden on 2 June, in Saitama, did little to match the intensity of England's build-up. Beckham began brightly and so did England as Sol Campbell rose to head home his skipper's expertly delivered corner on 23 minutes. Thereafter England chose bizarrely to retreat rather than force home the advantage against opponents bereft of cohesion and a clear game plan. Consequently, the Swedes gained a foothold in the game and profited from some sloppy England defending to equalise on the hour. Two minutes later, Beckham was withdrawn by Eriksson. The exertion of his first appearance in two months had clearly sapped the skipper's energy. Without him, the game petered out into a listless draw.

"The foot was aching a bit, but there's no problem," the captain said afterwards, dismissing fears that the injury might force him to miss the eagerly-awaited Argentina showdown five days later.

One Argentinian midfielder was happy to fan the flames of an old controversy. A month before England's grudge match with Argentina, the wily Diego Simeone, Beckham's nemesis at France '98, publicly admitted conning the referee to get the Englishman sent off.

"I went in hard, didn't get the ball but kicked his leg. I know I crashed into his back," said Simeone, describing his clash with Beckham for a television interview. "When I tried to stand up he kicked me from behind. I took advantage of that."

But the threat of any further gamesmanship did not materialise on a balmy evening in Sapporo on

Pages 82/83: Beckham drills home the winning penalty against Argentina.
Right: He celebrates the moment that buried painful memories of World Cup '98.

7 June. In fact, Argentina did nothing to justify their reputation as one of the world's toughest and most accomplished sides. Conversely, England's performance was majestic.

Eriksson's midfield, led by Beckham and Nicky Butt, controlled possession and the tempo of the game with the sort of skill and composure so often lacking in England teams. Rio Ferdinand and Sol Campbell were steadfast in defence, Michael Owen was a constant menace in attack. It was the Liverpool striker who won a penalty in the 44th minute when he was tripped by Mauricio Pochettino. In one strike of a football, David Beckham had the opportunity to finally exorcise the ghosts of France '98.

"Please, don't take any penalties," Victoria had begged before England's departure to the Far East. For once, Beckham ignored his wife. For once, he was nervous about taking a penalty.

The Argentinians tried to put him off. Goalkeeper Pablo Cavallero told Beckham which way to shoot. Diego Simeone attempted to shake his hand.

But the England captain was not to be denied his moment of glory and revenge. He drove the ball low past Cavallero to score the only goal of the game and secure a famous victory for his country.

"As I was standing there, four years of flashbacks went through my mind," he confessed later. "I didn't look at the keeper, didn't concentrate on anything but the ball, but my mind kept racing. As soon as I hit the ball, my mind went blank. It was the release of everything."

England needed just a point against Nigeria five days later to be sure of a place in the second phase. With that in mind and perhaps suffering an inevitable feeling of anti-climax after the Argentina triumph, Beckham and co played out a dour goalless draw with the Nigerians in Osaka.

That set up a second-round tie with Denmark in Niigata on 15 June. The Danes had been in impressive form, beating France as they topped a tough group that also featured Uruguay and Senegal. But England cruised to a 3–0 win with goals from Rio Ferdinand, Michael Owen and Emile Heskey.

England were into the quarter-finals of the World Cup for the first time since 1990 and would play the winners of the tie between Belgium and Brazil.

"I'm not bothered whether we get Brazil or Belgium," said Beckham confidently.

His optimism would prove ill-founded. Predictably, Brazil beat Belgium to stand between England and the semi-finals. The skipper was fit to face Brazil in Shizuoka on 21 June despite renewed fears about the state of his foot after he received a knock in the Denmark game.

Eriksson's men started well and deservedly took the lead on 23 minutes as Michael Owen again demonstrated his coolness in front of goal. However, it took the Brazilians just a few minutes to turn the game on its head with goals either side of half-time.

A fully-fit Beckham would have carried the can for Rivaldo's equaliser. But, given that his very participation in the tournament was a near miracle, no blame should be apportioned to the England captain. Approaching the interval, England held a 1–0 advantage, but Beckham withdrew from a challenge with Brazilian full-back Roberto Carlos which he should have been favourite to win. The future world champions spirited the ball to the other end of the field where Rivaldo placed a precise finish beyond David Seaman's despairing grasp. In an instant, all England's endeavour had been undone, the energy sucked out of them.

After the break, Seaman misjudged Ronaldinho's speculative free-kick as Brazil took the lead. Even when Ronaldinho was harshly sent from the field on the hour for a challenge on Danny Mills, England failed to wrest the initiative from 10-man Brazil.

England's skipper later acknowledged that his team had passed up a golden opportunity.

"I thought we missed out that afternoon on a real chance of winning the World Cup," Beckham said later. "With all due respect to Brazil, it wasn't as if we'd lost the game so much as handed it over."

But Beckham had led his country with style and composure. His determination to get fit for the finals evidenced his unstinting commitment.

Shortly after England's exit, Beckham expressed his confidence that England would win the European Championships in 2004. What nobody realised was that by the time Euro 2004 came around, David Beckham would have swapped Manchester for Madrid.

Habitual nemesis (and future team-mate) Roberto Carlos commiserates with Beckham after England crash out to 10-man Brazil at the quarter-final stage.

the
distance
between us

Victoria Beckham once informed the nation on live television, "He likes to borrow my knickers." Heaven only knows what Sir Alex Ferguson made of Posh Spice's revelation regarding the man she calls "Goldenballs".

Doubtless for a manager who frequently attempts to dampen media interest in his players, such publicity-seeking was anathema, an excruciating experience akin to pulling teeth.

Ferguson had often been concerned by what he regarded as the union of two opposites, the worlds of professional sport and show business.

"The showbiz element in his life, made inevitable by the pop-star status of his wife, Victoria, has sometimes caused me to worry about a possible threat to his chances of giving maximum expression to his huge talent," wrote the Manchester United manager in his autobiography, *Managing My Life*.

Before the notoriously ostentatious Posh and Becks wedding in the summer of 1999, Ferguson was alarmed by David's tendency to travel long distances to be with Victoria before returning to Manchester just in time for training the next morning. And by the early weeks of the new millennium, Ferguson needed all his players to be wide-awake. Leeds United were beginning to pose a genuine threat to United's title aspirations and it was essential the Manchester side claim at least a draw at Elland Road on Sunday 20 February.

As Ferguson prepared his squad for the crucial trip, there occurred one of several major flashpoints in his relationship with Beckham. On the Thursday before the fixture Brooklyn awoke apparently suffering from gastroenteritis.

Concerned about his child's welfare, Beckham rang United's Carrington training ground and left a message to say that he would miss training to tend his sick son. Ferguson was incensed and his anger compounded when pictures of Victoria attending a charity fashion show on the Thursday evening appeared in Friday's papers.

The manager immediately dropped Becks and fined him two weeks' wages, £50,000. According to Beckham, the manager gave him "the biggest dressing-down I've ever had." This included the accusation that David was "babysitting while your wife was out gallivanting."

There is a long-held perception – vehemently denied by Beckham – that his wife is the driving force and decision-maker in their relationship. Ferguson interpreted the entire incident as just another example of Victoria's unhealthy influence on his player. After all, the manager would have reasoned, it was surely not David's decision that the Beckham family would occasionally stay down in Hertfordshire meaning he would often have to get up at 6am to travel the 160 miles north for training.

While Beckham sat in the stands, baseball cap pulled low over his face, his team-mates delivered a stinging blow to the Yorkshire club's title pretensions. A combination of good fortune, excellent goalkeeping from the otherwise erratic Mark Bosnich and Andrew Cole's fine breakaway goal saw United cope in the absence of their number 7.

The Old Trafford truth police did their best to portray Beckham's omission as a run-of-the-mill disciplinary situation to be dealt with internally. In reality, and with hindsight, it was one of the crucial moments when the gap between player and manager opened up into a yawning chasm.

Above all, it represented a clash of cultures between the old-school football man and the modern father. Beckham had grown into the antithesis of the

Why does it always rain on me? Beckham's dissatisfaction with life at Old Trafford grew during his final two seasons at Manchester United.

traditional footballer: he preferred family life to nightlife, placing his wife and children above all else. Ironically, Ferguson would later admit in a magazine interview that he regretted not spending more time with his own family, especially when his children were young, because of his heavy work commitments. Perhaps, as parents sometimes do, Ferguson failed to realise that the boy to whom he had been a father figure had grown up into a man. And one who captained his country to boot. For the United boss admitted surprise at the way his former protégé prospered when given the England armband.

"I did not see him as a captain because he is a quiet lad. But he has done fantastically well the way he has fitted into the job with England – it has brought him on."

But according to Beckham, Ferguson didn't share the widespread enthusiasm for his match-winning performance against Greece in October 2001:

"The gaffer's first words to me were: 'I hope you're going to work bloody hard now you're back at United'."

In fairness to Ferguson, Beckham's game bore signs of fatigue after his exploits against Greece and the manager was forced to rest him for six of the eight games played in December.

15 February 2003, saw a watershed in Manchester United history on two fronts. The Old Trafford side crashed out of the FA Cup, losing 2–0 to Arsenal despite home advantage. The result paled into insignificance when it emerged what had occurred in the home dressing room in the immediate aftermath of the defeat.

A seething Ferguson accused Beckham of abicating his defensive responsibilities in the build-up to Arsenal's second goal. An argument ensued which culminated in Ferguson aiming an angry kick at a boot that was lying on the dressing-room floor. It flew at Beckham and caught him a glancing blow above his left eye, piercing the skin and causing him to bleed. By his own admission, Beckham snapped and went for Ferguson and team-mates Gary Neville, Ryan Giggs and Ruud van Nistelrooy had to restrain him.

"If I tried 100 times or a million times it could not happen again – if I could I would have carried on playing," Ferguson quipped regarding the accident.

Although both sides apparently moved to defuse the situation in public, Beckham deliberately made sure he was photographed with the cut above his eye in full view, slowing down in his car while leaving United's Carrington training complex.

"His body language, scowling, frowning but resolutely silent, made clear that much more than his eye had been wounded," wrote biographer Andrew Morton in his book, *Posh and Becks*.

The FA Cup defeat to Arsenal brought back painful memories of United's capitulation in the title race at home to the Gunners the previous May. The 2001/2002 season was a difficult one at Old Trafford. In the summer of 2001 the club had splashed out almost £50 million to bring Ruud van Nistelrooy and Juan Sebastian Veron to Manchester for what was supposed to be Ferguson's final tilt at the European Cup before retirement.

Van Nistelrooy was an instant hit, scoring 36 goals in 44 appearances. Veron, meanwhile, was a disappointment but, in mitigation, he was often hampered by injury and bravely attempted to play through the pain barrier.

Bizarrely though, Ferguson decided at the beginning of the season to offload his best centre-half Jaap Stam to Lazio, and bring in veteran French defender Laurent Blanc as a replacement. The Frenchman showed flashes of his class, but his ageing legs could not handle the pace and the move was ultimately a failure.

The speculation regarding Ferguson's successor hung over the club for much of the season, with Sven-Göran Eriksson and Martin O'Neill being the names most often mentioned. Finally, Ferguson did an about-turn and signed a new contract, delaying his retirement indefinitely.

United had started 2002 in fifth place but a brilliant run of four wins in five games meant they ended January top of the pile. February saw three wins out of three, but things began to go wrong in March. First United failed to beat relegation-bound Derby County before losing at home to Middlesbrough three weeks later and dropping to second in the Premiership.

All the while, Arsenal were just off the lead with the cushion of two games in hand. United tried

Looking back in anger: "Bootgate" ruptured the father-son relationship between Beckham and Sir Alex Ferguson which was already near breaking point.

desperately to stay in the race but their best efforts were in vain. On a personal level, Beckham enjoyed a rich vein of goalscoring form that saw him net 11 times in the league and five times in Europe, the best season return of his career.

However, there was still a nagging sensation that his best form of the campaign had been seen when he was playing for England, not for his club.

The final day of the season has often been a joyous occasion at Old Trafford in recent years. But on 11 May 2002, three days after surrendering the title to Arsenal, there was little cause for celebration. Even so, the club did manage to produce a symbol that apparently augured well for the future.

Before United kicked off against Charlton, Beckham appeared on the pitch as it was announced he had finally signed a new contract, ending 18 months of negotiations and rumours that he was set to move abroad.

The midfielder had roundly rejected such suggestions in an interview with the club's official magazine two months earlier. "United fans will never lose me," he promised.

So, why the saga surrounding his new contract?

"Like anyone's job, whether it's me or someone who works at a supermarket it's got to be right," Beckham replied, apparently oblivious to the fact that supermarket workers spend very little time in contract negotiations.

The new three-year, £15-million deal was certainly good news for Mr and Mrs Beckham. Even before signing the new contract, Beckham was rated football's second highest earner behind Zinedine Zidane. The French midfield genius was raking in £8.7 million annually. Before his enhanced club contract was signed, Beckham was earning £6.6 million. His new club earnings of £90,000 a week, including £20,000 for "image rights", catapulted him into first place.

Image rights – Beckham's share of profits made by Manchester United from merchandise bearing his name – were the sticking point in the negotiations. And the fact that this was such an issue was clear evidence that United regarded Beckham as a crucial element of their commercial activities.

However, the financial rewards seemed incongruous

with many of Beckham's performances on the pitch for his club. Match-going fans regarded Roy Keane, Paul Scholes and Ruud van Nistelrooy as far more influential players, but only the Irishman earned as much as Beckham.

In football, as in politics, it is impossible to please all of the people all of the time. David Beckham's metamorphosis from villain to national hero came at a cost. Sir Alex Ferguson was not the only person to believe that the incredible energy and commitment Beckham was putting into his England performances hampered his ability to perform at the very highest level for his club. During his last two seasons at Manchester United, many Old Trafford regulars discerned a general dip in form that was not apparent when he took the field with England.

Also, his new-found popularity with England fans was hard for the United faithful to swallow, especially since they had defended Beckham so vehemently against these people in his darkest hour. Yet Beckham seemed to be courting the very people who had once directed such appalling hatred against him and his family.

Many United fans who watched Beckham play every week perceived his celebrity now far outweighed his football ability, or at least the form he was producing. And his status as national hero was a source of great irritation for United fans after the midfielder broke his foot. The entire focus of media attention was on whether or not Beckham would be fit to play for England in the World Cup. This ignored the fact that United would be without Beckham for the remainder of the season, including the European Cup semi-final showdown with Bayer Leverkusen.

At least Beckham was diplomatic enough to recognise this. "The focus seems to have been mainly around the World Cup, whereas I have been thinking about the United games I will be missing," the England captain reminded the nation.

On 1 September 2002, the Beckhams' second child, Romeo, was born. Quite why he was named Romeo is uncertain. Brooklyn, their first son, was rumoured (incorrectly) to have got his name from the place where he was conceived. Meanwhile, Beckham had already started work on his third autobiography, to be published in September

Beckham's new-found popularity with England fans was hard for the Man United faithful to stomach, as these were the people they had once defended him against.

2003, in which he would ultimately have his pound of flesh.

Beckham and his Manchester United team-mates suffered a dreadful start to the 2002/03 campaign. While Arsenal seemed invincible before Christmas, United lost to Bolton, Leeds and Manchester City. However, convincing victories over Liverpool, Arsenal and West Ham, at home, saw United claw their way from fourth on 1 December to second by just a point 13 days later. The successes over their title rivals were particularly sweet given an injury crisis that saw Beckham, Roy Keane, Rio Ferdinand and Nicky Butt all sidelined.

After back-to-back defeats against Blackburn and Middlesbrough, the Old Trafford side embarked upon an exhilarating run of form, starting with Beckham-inspired victories over Birmingham City and Sunderland around the turn of the year. In the course of the following three months, United sparkled as in days of old, completing seven wins and forcing two draws.

The goalscoring prowess of Ruud van Nistelrooy, above all, ensured United were level on points with Arsenal at the beginning of April with an equal number of games played. This was to be the decisive month in the championship race as United faced a fixture calendar that might have shaken the spirit from lesser teams.

First Liverpool were thrashed 4–0 at Old Trafford before a pulsating 6–2 humbling of Newcastle United at St. James' Park a week later. The trip to Highbury on 16 April was then billed as the title decider. The outcome, a 2–2 draw, suited United as the away team and preserved their lead at the top of the table, although Arsenal had a game in hand.

Blackburn Rovers proved stiff opponents three days later but eventually succumbed to the brilliance of Paul Scholes, who scored twice in a 3–1 victory. The England midfielder was on target again as United beat Spurs 2–0 at White Hart Lane to end April five points ahead of Arsenal, having played a game more. A week later it was all over as Arsenal crashed at home to Leeds United.

However, the most newsworthy statistic concerned David Beckham, who played just 24 minutes of those first three vital games in April, watching the

rest from the substitutes bench. His replacement, Ole Gunnar Solskjaer, did everything to repay his manager's faith, scoring three goals and creating the all-important equaliser at Highbury with, ironically, a pinpoint cross from the right wing.

The fact that Ferguson preferred the Norwegian ahead of the England captain for the most crucial games of the campaign was a blatant indication that Beckham no longer had a future at Old Trafford. However, that is a judgement made with hindsight. There is an argument, however, that at the time manager's selections were made purely on merit.

The main furore surrounded the decision not to select Beckham for the European Cup quarter-final second-leg against Real Madrid. Again, though, Ferguson's strategy was a logical one. Solskjaer was in magnificent form, crossing as well as Beckham and also offering the ability to beat an opponent in one-on-one situations. By contrast, the England captain was one of United's least effective players when they suffered a humiliating 3–1 reverse at the Santiago Bernabeu in early April. In fairness, he went into the game nursing a tight left hamstring, and he "felt it ping" taking a free-kick in the first five minutes. He battled on but had a stinker, completely missing the target when presented with a straightforward scoring opportunity in the second half.

The "flying boot" incident was clear evidence that the relationship between Beckham and his manager was now beyond repair. And it wasn't long before newspapers all over Europe started linking the Manchester United player with a move to a foreign club, perhaps Internazionale of Italy or, more likely, European champions Real Madrid.

The rumours began to escalate in March but Beckham was quick to laugh off the speculation.

"It never gets me down," he said on 24 March. "I know there will always be speculation about all players so I don't let anything get me down."

Madrid's chief transfer negotiator Jorge Valdano revealed that Beckham "looks like the next big project for us" after bringing Luis Figo, Zinedine Zidane and Ronaldo to the club in previous seasons. The story was reported in England just two days after Beckham's initial denial along with a quote

Beckham's serious demeanour in the closing stages of Manchester United's amazing 2002/03 Premiership comeback spoke of a man ready for a change.

from the midfielder, which read:

"Any player would be honoured to be spoken about by Real Madrid."

By the time Madrid had knocked United out of the European Cup on 23 April, the speculation had gathered further momentum. It was even reported that Beckham had met his agent, Tony Stephens, immediately after the Madrid game to discuss the possibility of a transfer.

The following week Madrid started their cat-and-mouse pursuit of Beckham in earnest by releasing an official statement denying interest in the player. "Contrary to speculation," it read, "we have no intention of negotiating his transfer."

The Spaniards' denial convinced nobody. It was exactly the same tactic Valdano and club president Florentino Pérez had used in their pursuit of Ronaldo from Internazionale the previous August.

Meanwhile, Victoria Beckham, as adept at spin as Alistair Campbell and Shane Warne combined, hinted that her husband was on the move. The former Spice Girl nodded when asked at a showbiz party in New York whether she was intending to move abroad in the near future.

Given Solskjaer's excellent form, Beckham's own poor performance at the Bernabeu and mounting speculation that he would join Real Madrid, it was little surprise Sir Alex Ferguson left him on the bench for the return leg.

With United trailing, Beckham came on for Veron and made a telling impact, scoring with a trademark free-kick and a tap-in as the home side eventually triumphed 4–3 on the night. The England captain milked the ovation of the Old Trafford faithful after the final whistle. "I went to the four corners of the ground to return the applause," he wrote in his latest autobiography, *My Side*.

It is understandable that a man who felt cast aside by his club would be delighted to find he still had a place in the hearts of the fans. But the account of that night in Beckham's book makes no mention of the disappointment of again missing out on the trophy United covet above all others.

Instead, Beckham continues: "I went back to the house ... I decided not to wake the boys and tell them about Daddy's great night."

For everybody else associated with Manchester United the evening was one of shattered dreams; how could Beckham possibly refer to it as "Daddy's great night"?

For a second year running, United's final home league match of the season was against Charlton Athletic. Again, despite Ruud van Nistelrooy's hat-trick in a storming 4–1 victory, Beckham stole the headlines. An air of uncertainty hung around Old Trafford as the players saluted the fans who had cheered them to the verge of glory. Predictably, many television cameras were aimed at the England captain. "I've had talks," he appeared to mouth to best friend Gary Neville and the speculation regarding a move to Madrid went back into overdrive.

Beckham's final appearance for Manchester United was against Everton at Goodison Park as the season drew to a close. He marked his farewell with yet another deliciously struck free-kick to equalise Kevin Campbell's opener. Van Nistelrooy converted a second-half penalty as the champions maintained a run that saw them unbeaten in the league since the Boxing Day defeat to Middlesbrough.

It was United's seventh championship win in the nine seasons Beckham had been in the first team. He gained his first winners' medal in 1996, when Eric Cantona inspired United to the Double despite the sale of Mark Hughes, Paul Ince and Andrei Kanchelskis.

Having witnessed the departure of those great players, Beckham realised that the club would always be bigger than any of the individuals who represented it:

"No one is ever allowed to get too big-time at United. At Old Trafford, you have to remember that all the big players leave and the club goes on."

There was no concerted outcry from hardcore Manchester United fans at the possible sale of Beckham. When the midfielder finally joined the Spanish champions for £25 million, the mood in the letters pages of United fanzines was one of relief. As one supporter wrote to *United We Stand*:

"Gradually, he [Beckham] went from a player who you could tolerate off the pitch because of his on-field excellence, to one whose priority no longer seemed to be United."

Always the first player to acknowledge Manchester United fans' support, Beckham's gestures became more emotional as his Madrid move beckoned.

the
man
who went to
madrid

Heathrow Airport, 17 June 2003. As David and Victoria Beckham stride towards their departure gate to board a flight for Tokyo accompanied by a battery of photographers and television camera crews, he suddenly feels his mobile phone begin to vibrate in the palm of his hand. It is his agent Tony Stephens with the news the couple have been waiting to hear for months.

"I bet there are cameras pointed at you right now, aren't there?" says Stephens. "Well, just be sure you and Victoria realise they're taking the first pictures, of you both walking in to a new adventure, a new world, together. It's all agreed. Enjoy yourselves." Beckham turns to his wife and whispers: "It's done."

After months of relentless speculation that had dominated the British summer, David Beckham was finally a Real Madrid player. Stephens had swiftly agreed another lucrative contract for his client after Manchester United had accepted a bid of close to £25 million.

According to Beckham's version of events, which he details in his latest autobiography *My Side*, the final decision to join Real Madrid was taken less than 40 hours before he took that call from Stephens at Heathrow. On Sunday 15 June, he had invited his and Victoria's families to their house in Hertfordshire to enjoy a barbecue and help decide where he would be playing his football next season.

"Everyone is here to help us with the hardest choice we'd ever had to make," writes Beckham of that afternoon. "Stay in Manchester and sign that new contract? Or leave England? And for where?" During the day he phones Manchester United's chief executive Peter Kenyon and gains the impression he is no longer wanted at Old Trafford, before phoning the Real Madrid President Florentino Perez an hour later, who tells him he is waiting for him with open arms. After their families have left, the Beckhams stay up late discussing their options until David picks up the phone and calls Stephens at two in the morning: "We've decided, it's Real Madrid."

The truth is Beckham had decided he was interested in a move to the Spanish capital a lot earlier than the middle of June. The thought of a new challenge in a foreign country and the breakdown of his relationship with Sir Alex Ferguson had made him start looking beyond Old Trafford from around the turn of the year, and so he was naturally delighted to learn as early as the beginning of April that Real Madrid had begun to sound out his management company, SFX about a move to the Bernabeu.

On the final day of the 2002/03 season, after Manchester United have lifted the Premiership trophy at Goodison Park, Beckham has reflected: "If you'd asked me that afternoon if I was leaving United, I'd have told you: "Not in a million years … I didn't want to leave." Three days later, on 14 May, he was given the opportunity to fulfil that ambition when Manchester United offered him a new four-year contract, which contained a generous pay-rise. However, Beckham showed little interest in signing it.

This new contract seems to rather undermine the story Beckham would stick to all summer that he never wanted to leave United and was forced out of Old Trafford. In *My Side*, he deals with the offer of a new contract in an utterly unconvincing manner, writing "I know some supporters probably thought: 'If you want to stay at Old Trafford, why don't you just sign it?'." But then he fails to answer this very question and attempts to brush over it.

"All of a sudden, they stuck a new contract in front of me as if to say: sign this or forget it … The only reason I'd ever leave United is if I could see they wanted me to. Well, at the moment it feels like

First steps of a new adventure. Beckham quickly got into the routine of being a Madrid player

they're not really bothered either way." Not bothered? Manchester United had just offered him a contract, which raised his wages from £90,000 to £100,000 a week only a year after he had signed his last contract. Strangely, Beckham goes on to claim, "This wasn't a situation I was in control of anyway."

In the following weeks, Beckham has admitted that Tony Stephens held meetings with several clubs in Europe. On 24 May, he had lunch in Nice with Joan Laporta, a candidate in the forthcoming Barcelona presidential elections, who was keen to use the signing of Beckham to help him win power, and then on 2 June Stephens flew to Madrid for two days of secret talks with Real Madrid.

It is against this backdrop that Beckham, on holiday with his family in the United States, gives an interview to *The Los Angeles Times* in which he says, "I'm a Manchester United player. As long as they want me, I'll stay." The powerbrokers at Old Trafford were absolutely furious; Beckham had been given the opportunity to remain at Old Trafford with the offer of a new contract, but he had failed to show any interest in signing it, and instead had allowed his agent to begin hawking him across Europe.

It dawns on United, who have also been conducting their own discreet discussions with Barcelona and Real Madrid to cover themselves if Beckham decides to leave, that he is highly unlikely to sign the new contract. United accelerate these talks and on 10 June announce they have accepted a £30 million bid from Joan Laporta, conditional on his election as president of Barcelona.

It is a foolish move by United as it gives the impression that they are forcing Beckham out of Old Trafford against his will. It is an absolute gift in the propaganda war that is being played out on the back pages of the newspapers, and Beckham milks it for all its worth.

"Was I in earthquake country?" he innocently pleads in *My Side* about the moment Stephens informs him United have accepted Laporta's bid. "I couldn't believe what I was hearing. No word from the gaffer, no word from anybody at the club, after a dozen years at United … I was angry all right. I didn't like the news, and how I'd found out about it, some time after the rest of the world, was humiliating …

I wasn't just up for sale, I'd been carted as far as the checkout. Something inside me shifted."

Stephens and his team at SFX quickly rushed out a press statement that read: "David is very disappointed and surprised to learn of this statement and feels that he has been used as a political pawn in the Barcelona Presidential elections. David's advisors have no plans to meet Mr Laporta."

Of course, SFX had conveniently forgotten to mention that they had already met Laporta, and had no more interest in dealing with him as Beckham was only interested in moving to Real Madrid. Beckham's apparently imminent arrival at the Bernabeu was an open secret in Spain for months, with another candidate in the Barcelona presidential elections, Jaume Llaurado claiming "Beckham's not coming [to Barcelona]. He signed for Madrid on 12 May."

But this didn't stop Beckham fuelling the erroneous idea that he was the betrayed and wounded party, nothing more than a dumb animal at a cattle auction. It brought him a wave of sympathy; *The Mirror* branding Sir Alex Ferguson as a "Red Bully" on their front page and wailing, "What a way to treat an England hero!", while the PFA's chief executive Gordon Taylor jumped to Beckham's defence, saying: "United are showing absolutely no loyalty for someone who has done so much for the club. I wouldn't sell a second-hand car like this and they are treating Beckham like a piece of horse meat – trading him off with no feeling."

Pieces of meat don't normally have the choice of signing a multi-million pound contract with either Manchester United, Barcelona or Real Madrid, but even on 15 June, the day Beckham has said he finally decided to join Madrid, his camp couldn't stop spinning the line that he was being forced out of Old Trafford. Beckham was quoted in the *News of the World* as saying, "I'd rather pack in football than leave Manchester United," before adding the utterly ridiculous claim that, "I'll prove to Alex Ferguson my loyalty for the club by playing for free if I have to."

Forty-eight hours later, Beckham had completely forgotten about his desperation to stay at United and play for free by agreeing to join Real Madrid. By this stage, the sale was welcomed by both him and United, who realised he could leave for nothing in two years, but it was Beckham who was determined to avoid being seen as its instigator. It does Beckham little credit that he was not brave enough to admit he wanted to join Madrid, a move he would later describe as, "a dream come true".

The day after the move was announced, a source at Real Madrid was quoted in *The Guardian* as saying, "David Beckham agreed personal terms with Real Madrid long in advance of Tuesday's announcement. As early as the start of May he had already fixed a salary, a home and a school for his children in Spain. The two clubs hadn't made a deal but Beckham was very determined to move to Real Madrid."

Two weeks later, after Beckham had returned from his promotional tour to the Far East, he headed straight to Madrid to complete the transfer. On 2 July he was paraded in front of 600 members of the world's media as a Real Madrid player, and greeted by the Madrid president Florentino Perez, who called him "an icon of our time and of our planet". Beckham made a very short speech, no more than 50 words, before he was handed the Number 23 shirt by Real Madrid's greatest ever player Alfredo Di Stefano.

What sort of player had Real Madrid bought for £25 million? Despite captaining England and enjoying a constant stream of success at Old Trafford, Beckham's standing in the game continues to be fiercely debated. There is a large swell of opinion within the game which refuses to buy into the argument Beckham is a great player. And surely this is the very definition of greatness: your talent is beyond debate; no one argues over Diego Maradona or Pele, just as they don't with today's greats, Beckham's new team-mates Zinedine Zidane and Ronaldo. Genuine greatness is accepted, not dismissed and maligned as regularly as Beckham has been.

When Diego Maradona watched Beckham's performances at last year's World Cup he had this to say: "Fame is gauged on what you do on the pitch. Beckham scored a penalty [against Argentina] that shouldn't have been and England went out in the quarter-finals. That's no reason to go out and buy a Beckham shirt."

Indeed, when Barcelona bid for Beckham in the

summer of 2003, one of their players, the Swedish international Patrik Anderson, who won the Champions League with Bayern Munich in 2001, felt confident enough to say, "There are at least 20 players in the world who are better in his position ... Beckham is not someone who can beat a man one-on-one."

And this has always been the trump card for Beckham cynics; he lacks what the Italians call *fantasia*, the ability to glide past players with either pace or trickery. Beckham is perceived to be too predictable out on the right flank, and the type of player accomplished defences found relatively simple to snuff out.

Beckham might still have some way to go to be recognised as one of football's all-time greats, but at Manchester United he has earned a place in their pantheon of legends. A swift glance over Beckham's eight seasons in the first team at Old Trafford should convince even his most entrenched sceptic that he deserves to keep the company of Bobby Charlton, George Best and Duncan Edwards. In his 399 games for United Beckham scored 88 goals and provided a constant supply of moments to cherish; his winner in the 1996 FA Cup semi-final against Chelsea at Villa Park; that goal from the halfway line for United against Wimbledon at Selhurst Park which hinted at what was to come; those wonderful crosses, most famously in the dying minutes against Bayern Munich in the Champions League final for Sheringham and Solskjaer to score from; goals against Tottenham on the final day of the season in the Premiership and Arsenal in that classic FA Cup semi-final replay to keep United's hopes of the Treble alive before they had even reached Barcelona. He left United with a swag bag containing six Premiership title medals, two FA Cup winners' medals and a Champions League winners' medal.

It was his performances in a red shirt that led to him twice being voted runner-up in the World Footballer of the Year poll, in 1999 and 2001, and had the greats of the game he hopes to emulate lining up to praise him. Pele has said, "I love the way Beckham plays ... If I were a coach I would always want him in my team." Johan Cruyff has said, "He thrills me, he is one of the elite," while Franz

Beckenbauer declared, "He's a world-class player, maybe the best of all."

The debate about whether Beckham is one of football's greats or just another pretender will continue to rage, but what is certain is that he has become more than just a footballer; he is a sporting and cultural icon, recognised across the globe.

Beckham spent most of the summer of 2003 attempting to exploit this on what seemed to be an endless world tour, first attempting to establish himself in the USA and then on a promotional tour of the Far East. As he made his way through Thailand, Japan, Malaysia and Vietnam, Beckham sparked scenes of fan devotion reminiscent of the Beatles in their prime, with tens of thousands greeting him at airports and following his every move. The ten-day trip earned Beckham an estimated £10 million.

The trip across the Atlantic might not have been nearly as successful, but the idea that Beckham, a mere English "soccer" player, thought he had a chance of becoming famous in North America shows the size of his rampant fame. Beckham failed to "break" the US, but he did manage to prick Americans' curiosity; he was interviewed on network television, featured on the cover of the leading magazine *Men's Journal* as "The Most Famous Athlete in the World" and given the chance to present an award at the MTV Movie Awards with his wife. No doubt it would have been noted by an increasingly agitated Sir Alex Ferguson that while Beckham was flouncing down a red carpet in Hollywood, Roy Keane was studying for his UEFA B coaching badge on a 10-day intensive course at Warwick University.

"I think there's an anticipation that Beckham's potential is endless," said the American sports promoter Charlie Stillitano. "Americans always feel that they have the biggest and the best and the last time we didn't have that was probably Pele. We have Michael Jordan, Tiger Woods and Muhammad Ali and now there's a keen understanding that the most famous athlete in the world is not an American. I don't see any reason why Beckham could not be on a par with these people."

But while Ali was the greatest ever boxer, Jordan, the greatest ever basketball player and Woods is already considered the greatest ever golfer, Beckham would struggle to make the Top 100 all-time greatest footballers. He is arguably the most famous ever footballer, but the best? Never.

Beckham's iconic status has been the triumph of hype over talent. His overwhelming global fame has been earned, not as Ali and Jordan's were, for their sporting genius, but for his model-looks and ability to package himself as a "celebrity". Despite being a Beckham fan, Pele himself observed, "Beckham is more of a pop star than a footballer."

Beckham's ceaseless self-promotion and his willingness to be hawked around as a "brand" alongside his wife seems to be something of a soulless and cynical exercise. Listen to Victoria Beckham when asked in America in the summer of 2003 what they had to offer as a couple: "We want to have our own brand. There are so many things that interest us, fashion, make-up. I'm kind of looking at the big picture now and thinking 'Yes, the music's great, but this is about the big picture.' There are so many areas you could hit."

There appears to be precious little substance behind the Beckham phenomenon. He is the perfect icon for the 21st century; bland and safe, someone you can project anything you want onto. He will not cause offence or offer an opinion; he recently admitted that he had never voted and had no interest in politics.

It shocked some to learn that Beckham is even provided with set answers to questions that may or may not be asked in interviews or press conferences. A dossier called the "DB Asia Tour Bible", produced for Beckham by his agents at SFX, was found by a Japanese reporter in Tokyo. It provided a fascinating insight it to just how controlled Beckham is. He was provided with scripted answers to even the most simple and banal questions, for example if asked: "How is your Spanish?" He was told to answer, "Limited apart from reading menus full of paella or sangria. But I'm a quick learner."

One question asked about how he felt at being "sold" by United to Barcelona without his knowledge. He answered honestly and said he wasn't happy with it. Hours later he was made to look like a disobedient child when SFX issued a retraction saying that he

The reign in Spain. Beckham's popularity with young fans appears identical in Madrid to how it was in Manchester.

was actually fine with it after all.

In a story headlined, "Whatever happened to nice boy Becks?" Matt Lawton of the *Daily Mail*, who followed Beckham on this tour, wrote: "The England captain we admire for the way he put his life and career back together following the 1998 World Cup has been lost somewhere in a sea of sycophancy and commercial jargon. He has been cast adrift from reality, a marketing image whose ability as a footballer is almost secondary to the fashion and style icon who can sell anything from face cream to parts for second-hand cars ... Beckham is a decent man, a terrific player and a fine England captain but, increasingly, those qualities are being forgotten."

At the end of July, David Beckham draws up in his car at the Bernabeu stadium to meet his new team-mates for the first time. "I got there early and just sat outside in the car, you don't want to be first in, do you, looking too keen?" he has said. "But you don't want to be last, either. It was like your first day at secondary school or something. When I finally decided it was the right time, the two other players who were already in the dressing room when I got there were Zidane and Ronaldo. I thought, 'They'll do for me'."

Beckham had to convince Madrid's fans and media that he deserved a place alongside these players. "Madrid watchers weren't completely convinced about Beckham when he signed," wrote *The Guardian*'s Madrid correspondent Sid Lowe. "The Englishman, many thought, was an effeminate pretty boy with silly hair, hardly likely to sweat for the cause ... They seemed incapable of truly believing in Beckham the committed team player."

Beckham acquitted himself well on Madrid's own trip to the Far East, and even scored on his debut, but these were mere pre-season games with little relevance. Back in Spain, when he had a quiet game in Madrid's 2–1 defeat against Real Mallorca in the first leg of the Spanish Super Cup, their version of the Community Shield, he was immediately dismissed in some quarters as not good enough. "Beckham looked like he did whenever Manchester United played in Spain," sneered the former Real Madrid player Michel, who is now a television commentator. "The Englishman couldn't adapt to Iberian pace, passion, pressure, or greatness."

But in the return leg, Beckham scored with a rare header as Madrid overcame Mallorca 3–0 to win the Super Cup, and then on his La Liga debut against Real Betis at the Bernabeu, he further silenced his critics after just 126 seconds with a simple tap-in; later he provided a wonderful pass for Zidane to set up Ronaldo for Madrid's second goal and win the game 2–0. You could see Beckham almost glow with a sense of belonging during the game as he swapped a succession of passes with Zidane in the middle of the pitch. Afterwards, he said, "This is the happiest I have been for 18 months."

In the very next game when Madrid found themselves losing 1–0 with only five minutes remaining away to Villareal it was Beckham who inspired the team and helped salvage a point. He got stuck in all over the pitch and provided the cross for Madrid's late equaliser. The Madrid press were beginning to warm to the Englishman. "Beyond the ad campaigns, the dyed hair, the changes of look, the premature autobiography and the famous singing wife, Beckham is making it plain that he is also a quite fabulous football player," declared the Madrid sports paper, *Marca*.

As Beckham continued to thrive in Madrid's 7–2 victory over Valladolid and 3–1 win over Malaga, the whole of Real Madrid, from the boardroom to the pitch, fell over themselves to gush about his talent although perhaps the real sign that the England captain had been accepted at the Bernabeu was the praise showered up on him by the club's spiritual leader and captain, Raul, "Beckham's arrival benefits me, thanks to his quality and his vision," he said. "The passes he gives are magnificent. He has started very well and has gained the respect of all."

While Beckham was deciding whether to move to Madrid in the Spring, one of the club's *galaticos* Roberto Carlos said something which deeply resonated with him: "A player can only be considered truly world class if he has played for Real Madrid in his career. Players like Figo, Zidane and Ronaldo came to Spain with big reputations but playing for Madrid has made their reputations greater." Over the next four, Beckham will be making sure the same happens to him.

Juggling skills. Beckham seems to have successfully, so far, managed both his playing career and off-pitch activities.

David Beckham statistics

1992/93

	Apps	Sub	Gls
Premiership	0	0	0
FA Cup	0	0	0
League Cup	0	1	0
Europe	0	0	0
TOTAL	0	1	0
International	0	0	0

1994/95

	Apps	Sub	Gls
Premiership	2	2	0
FA Cup	1	0	0
League Cup	3	0	0
Europe	1	0	1
TOTAL	7	2	1
International	0	0	0

1995/96

	Apps	Sub	Gls
Premiership	33	7	7
FA Cup	3	0	1
League Cup	2	0	0
Europe	2	0	0
TOTAL	40	7	8
International	0	0	0

1996/97

	Apps	Sub	Gls
Premiership	34	3	8
FA Cup	2	0	1
League Cup	0	0	0
Europe	9	0	2
TOTAL	45	3	11
International	8	1	0

1997/98

	Apps	Sub	Gls
Premiership	34	3	9
FA Cup	3	1	2
League Cup	0	0	0
Europe	8	0	0
TOTAL	41	4	11
International	7	2	1

1998/99

	Apps	Sub	Gls
Premiership	34	1	6
FA Cup	7	0	1
League Cup	0	1	0
Europe	11	0	2
TOTAL	52	2	9
International	5	0	0

1999/2000

	Apps	Sub	Gls
Premiership	30	1	6
FA Cup	0	0	0
League Cup	0	0	0
Europe	12	0	2
TOTAL	42	1	8
International	11	0	0

2000/01

	Apps	Sub	Gls
Premiership	29	2	9
FA Cup	2	0	0
League Cup	0	0	0
Europe	11	1	0
TOTAL	42	3	9
International	8	0	3

2001/02

	Apps	Sub	Gls
Premiership	23	5	11
FA Cup	1	0	0
League Cup	0	0	0
Europe	13	0	5
TOTAL	37	5	16
International	12	0	3

2002/03

	Apps	Sub	Gls
Premiership	27	4	6
FA Cup	3	0	1
League Cup	5	0	1
Europe	10	3	3
TOTAL	45	7	11
International	6	0	4

CAREER SUMMARY

	Apps	Sub	Gls
Premiership	246	28	62
FA Cup	22	1	6
League Cup	10	2	1
Europe	77	4	15
TOTAL	355	35	84
International	60	3	12

THE FACTS

Personal:
Born: 2 May 1975, Leytonstone
Height: 6 foot
Playing weight: 11st 2lbs
Position: Midfielder

Clubs:

MANCHESTER UNITED
Signed trainee: 8 July 1991
Signed professional: January 1993
Debut: v Brighton & Hove Albion (a),
23 September 1992, League Cup

PRESTON NORTH END
Signed (loan): March 1995
Debut: v Doncaster Rovers (h), 4 March 1995
Appearances (sub) /goals:
Division 3: 4 (1) / 2

REAL MADRID
Signed: 2 July 2003
Transfer fee: £25 million
Debut: v Real Betis (h), 30 August 2003
Appearances (sub) /goals
La Liga: 4 (0) / 2 goals
Champions League: 1 (0) / 0 goals

HONOURS

Team:
Premiership: 1996, 1997, 1999, 2000, 2001, 2003
FA Cup: 1996, 1999
European Cup: 1999

Personal:
PFA Young Player Of The Year: 1997
2nd World Footballer Of The Year: 1999, 2001
2nd European Footballer Of The Year: 1999

INTERNATIONAL RECORD
England (1996–):
60 (3) apps, 13 goals

statistics correct as at 21/9/03

"A player can only
be considered truly
world class if he
has played for
Real Madrid."

Roberto Carlos